Money Prick

The Harsh Truth Your Friends Don't Have

The Balls Or Brains To Tell You

I0492163

Published by Taylor Young at Smashwords
Copyright 2013 by Taylor Young
Cover by Vila Design

i

Introduction

The Harsh Truth

Chances are, since you're reading this book, you are sometimes a fool with your money. A downright asshole. You're probably afraid to add up all the money you've blown like a drunken sailor on shore leave. And maybe you're thinking it's time to change all of that.

This book is precisely the knock upside the numbskull that you need. I hope to insult you like a big prick until you either throw my book in the dumpster or put down your pride and admit that a lot of these tips are right on the mark.

Let's cut to the chase. Would you drag yourself to work and put up with the office dramas and divas and all their bullshit if it wasn't for that pathetic paycheck? I wouldn't either. But most of us are going to have to work long hours every day, every week, until we're old because we're spending all we make and more (going into debt) buying way more crap than we need.

We are slaves in a free land. Ironic, isn't it? Then, to add insult to injury, we're spending most of our spare time taking care of all the shit we don't even have the time to enjoy.

If you want real freedom to do the things that really matter the most to you, then you're going to have to grow a backbone and some larger gonads to go with it. It takes some guts to tell yourself and your family to lose the fascination with buying stuff and borrowing money. The spending frenzy has to fuck off.

Emotions will fly high when you cut back, down size and sell off a butt load of your crap. It takes some "fuck the system" attitude to live a simpler lifestyle while everyone around you pathetically lives beyond their means trying to look rich.

You need a name change. You can no longer be "the Jones" or their wannabe neighbor. Instead, be the quiet but sly as a fox neighbor that becomes loaded and no one saw it coming. The tips for getting there are cunningly presented in the insulting bitch slapping dialogues that follow. Please get pissed off by them.

<nobolz4IOU$$>

Chapter 1

Big Ugly Lawn Ornaments

While many people adore motor homes and campers, they are not my thing. In fact, my wife and I hate them and the airheads driving them. It's especially annoying when we're stuck behind one while trying to speed down a road with no chance to pass.

Although Hollywood has created some hilarious movies with RV's (Recreational Vehicle) as the stage, in reality they are very expensive to operate and own. It's much cheaper to simply go enjoy them at the movie theatre. In fact, it's actually cheaper to burn a few hundred dollar bills every day.

A "rolling house on wheels" is an awful investment. Really, investment is the wrong word since investments are supposed to go up in value. Motor home and camper values drop like a rock the minute you drive or pull them off the lot. A new RWV (Reverse Wealth Vehicle) is intended for people who can't do math or are so rich they don't care about the math. Would you buy a house knowing it would drop half of its value in a few years?! You gotta be rich or rash or both to do this.

The cost for maintenance, licensing, insurance, and fuel is jaw dropping too. If the RWV is not motorized, it takes a beast of a truck to pull it. Either way, going on a trip is like running hundred dollar bills through a paper shredder, then burning them just to be sure they are toast. All this just because you don't want to sleep in a motel bed? Granted, motel beds are a little nasty, but a can of Lysol spray is a lot cheaper than a camper. Get over it.

It takes time to groom these big monsters too. People have to clean them before and after a trip, then figure out where and how to store them for the winter. Hmm, this sounds like a lot of time sucking work to me!

What is wrong with the good old-fashioned approach to travel, such as a seedy motel room, cramped pop-up camper, or simply a tent and a musty sleeping bag? At least consider other means of family fun that don't involve so much time and expense before you do take the RWV plunge.

Sell the RV, unless you use it all the time and it's paid for. And think twice about buying an RV unless you 1) can pay cash for it, 2) found a steal on a used one, and 3) plan to live in it or use it most weekends. Only buy if the answer to all three criteria is "yes."

If you can really afford an RV and enjoy using it, great! We're not against that. But if you buy an RWV and can't afford it, then you're just hauling your financial problems around the country or have a very expensive lawn ornament covered by an ugly tarp like our pathetic neighbors do. Don't do it.

<nobolz4IOU$$>

Chapter 2

The Macho Effect

Too many "men" trade their family's security for their manly big rig image. Don't believe me? How many guys do you know who sold their tripped out 4X4 diesel pickup and bought a beater economy car to save money for the emergency fund or kid's college fund?

Look around any parking lot. Pay attention to what's driving down nearly every street. They're everywhere - beasts like those hideous Hummers and other big ball rigs. My wife calls these overblown vehicles "compensation rigs." These big muscle rigs are oversized to balance out something that is lacking. Like brains, a backbone…or a dick!

And ladies, if this fairy tale hits close to home then maybe you should wake up from your trashy romance novel trance too. Women blow their share of money on "need something dependable" rigs every bit as much. Whenever I see these full size SUVs choking the streets around town and crossing into my lane at every curve, like the drivers have a thumb up their rear end, I always figure it's a woman driving. No offense, girls, but maybe some orange cones and an abandoned parking lot are in order.

Now there's nothing wrong with buying an impressive set of wheels, if you can afford them. And that is the problem. Too many people who buy these impressive rigs can't afford them. Really - who can afford them? Only the rich and I can assure you, there aren't that many rich people out there.

Listen up. Women have a strong need to feel safe and able to take care of the kids. That usually translates to having a hefty emergency savings. This creates a conflict. These big rigs soak up a lot of money. As in tons of money--one of the biggest killers of wealth building.

So don't let a fancy rig wreak financial havoc on your family. Put down your pride and swap the "ego rig" for an "eco rig." That is macho.

<nobolz4IOU$$>

Chapter 3

Hazard Pay

You cannot use someone else's money risk-free. No? You'd have less risk putting on a used condom.

Some ballsy folks borrowed money at a low-interest rate and invested it in the stock market, hoping to make a killing. They were confident that they wouldn't get burned, since the math says borrowing at 4% and getting a return of 8% percent in the stock market is a win of 4%, right? In theory, yes. But in actual practice, a big spanking no.

If you don't factor in the risk of investments but look only at the math, then you're probably one of those drivers who's got one of their thumbs up their ass and is always in everyone's way. You have to factor in the risk, which could cause the expected 4% win to suddenly nose dive to a negative "return." Even experts cannot predict what the stock market will do. A market dip could cause you to lose it all or even go in the hole.

But then we hear, "I'm not putting my money at risk; I'm using the bank's money to make money." Really! And New Mexico is in Mexico, right? If the bank loses their money, then they'll be coming for your house or whatever you listed as collateral.

Or are you one of those people willing to take a risk and then just walk away or go bankrupt and stiff everyone else, including your grandkids? Look, if you really need to stiff someone, go find a whore and leave the rest of us out of it.

If you have money to burn and want to take risks with it, then go ahead. But unless you can afford to throw money out the window, then don't fall for any get-rich-quick schemes. The odds of winning are very low – you have a much better chance of catching a disease in Vegas.

<nobolz4IOU$$>

Chapter 4

Play For The Greenbacks

The simplest and most powerful thing you can do with your money is to decide to keep some of every dollar for yourself. Go on, be selfish and keep some of your money to yourself. It's by far better than robbing your kids and grandkids like you currently are with your out of control debt, foreclosures and bankruptcy.

Wouldn't it be great to pay yourself each month, instead of seeing it fly away to everyone else? What if you could give yourself a raise? You can, you dick wad. That's what we're talking about!

Every time you get paid another clash begins. Really. Everyone else is competing to rip the greenbacks out of your hands like relatives at Uncle Pete's final will reading. They're winning more than you are, and you're getting beat up during the skirmishes. In fact, you're getting your ass kicked. But you can lick your wounds and turn the game back in your favor.

Get fucking mad enough to do something about it. Get that determination going. Become smart about the ways you are being separated from your money. If only the girlfriends of your youth would have given up their virginity as easily as you give up your money, then you might have something to really talk about. But no, you lost out on both.

So start paying attention from the moment that you are paid. Keep on a look out for interceptions, turnovers, and fumbles. As you figure out ways to increase your "score," you'll learn to love the game. Once you start winning at it, it is so damn fun.

So let the game begin!

<nobolz4IOU$$>

Chapter 5

Four-Wheeled Love Affair

We love our cars and trucks. A tough truck, sleek luxury car, or classic muscle car is a thing of beauty. The look, feel, and smell of s new rig is exciting, and can bring a smile to even the grouchiest person's face. Too bad the smell is simply toxic fumes being released into the air….and that would explain the stupid grin on our face and why our math skills disappear after test-driving a new rig.

To replace that shit eating grin on your face with a sly smile, here are some "rules of the road."

Trading in your "barely used" rig every few years for a new one is the recipe for a blown job evacuation plan (retirement). Don't believe me? Most people don't pay off an auto loan before getting another one. It doesn't take long before they owe more on their current vehicle than it is worth. Then it seems there's no choice but to keep rolling the "old" car debt into the "new" car loan. Here's where bad math, poor planning, and a low IQ collide.

New cars are more dependable and that makes the car loan worth it…or so the fairy tale goes. In reality an older, well-maintained rig is just as dependable as a flashy, new rig. And that older rig leaves the owner with money to treat the gang for dinner at a favorite restaurant and fund a flashy job evacuation plan, too.

"What about the warranty" you're sputtering? That warranty is small consolation when that shiny SUV (which is still sporting a paper license taped to the rear window) leaves you stranded along the expressway, at midnight during a thunderstorm. And just when you think your luck can't get any worse, there won't be cell phone coverage to call for a tow.

Believe me, I've driven plenty of old cars lots of miles – it's no more risky than a new car that is poorly designed or loaded with electronic toys (just waiting to betray you). You still have to do maintenance on both or you'll be stranded.

Don't dump a rig that's just getting broken in. Wait until the mechanic's bill is more than what the car is worth to you, or until the rig starts acting flaky like a pastry. Then go enjoy a fresh pastry and lose the stale rig.

When it's time to replace a vehicle, buy one that's at least three years old and only had one owner. The fastest thing about a new car is how it loses value (as much as 20%) when driven off the dealer's lot. It should also freak you out that in five years your new prize will likely be worth only half of what you paid for it.

And don't pat yourself on the back because you bought a new economy car either – you're still throwing away a hundred dollar bill every month for five years! Let someone else take the hit in the shorts.

People dump lemons quickly, so owner "hopping" is the call sign of a problem car. Avoid multiple owner cars that are relatively new.

Avoid rental and fleet cars, since they are driven hard. "But they do great maintenance on them," your pie hole says. Ever see a "drive it like you just stole it" bumper sticker? Ever see an adult become a teenager again behind the wheel of a rented car? Consistent maintenance can only do so much for a rig that has been driven "off-road" style.

Just how many vehicles does your family need anyway? Sell a "rarely used" rig and don't replace it. Use this money to jump start your emergency fund. Or replace a newer rig with one that's a few years more loved. Unless you regularly move heavy things, sell the truck. Borrow or rent a "beast" whenever it's needed.

If you want to keep the rigs you have, pay off the loans (if you have them) as quickly as possible. Then keep the rig and continue making the car payment—this time to your savings. Replace the rig down the road with cash. If you always make car payments to yourself, you may miss out on needing a vehicle loan ever again. Now that will be sweet driving, huh?

<nobolz4IOU$$>

Chapter 6

Uncommon Cents

Why do we rush out to blow our paycheck as soon as it hits our bank account? The bank has barely posted the deposit before we are impulse buying all over town like your Uncle Jack's string of booze purchases and Saturday night whores. A jaw-dropping amount of our wage goes toward frivolous stuff, rather than being nurtured like a prize.

This proves that common sense is not common when it comes to money. Otherwise the largest wealth building tool available to us—our paycheck—would be protected as diligently as we worked to earn it.

Chances are you have lots of experience spending money, but haven't spent much time learning how to hold on to it. If you spent half the time thinking about money as you do thinking with your dick, no, a quarter the time, you'd have this money thing licked by now.

So here's the bottom line on this irony. If you ever want to stop having to work someday, then you better start saving like you want to stop working someday.

<nobolz4IOU$$>

Chapter 7

Bailing Out

Tough love is so hard to carry out. Even if your kids moan and argue bitterly otherwise, parents carry the most challenging role of enforcing the "rules." If we lived in a different universe then maybe parents would eat the endless ice cream without gaining a pound....and the little spoiled brats would get the grey hair, wrinkles, and never have time for their video games.

There's a slippery slope between being a safety net and being an enabler. Your heart screams out to fix your kids mistakes so they do not have to pay any idiot tax. And your head boldly argues to let them wallow in their small shit holes, so they will learn to not fall into the bigger cesspools later. If you haven't figured this out yet, your head should win this argument, not your precious feelings or big heart.

When kids are bailed out of trouble, they usually don't learn a damn thing, except that they can get away with being little ass wipes. So we end up bailing them out again...and again. Eventually they become old enough to know better, and yet still haven't grown up. They become even bigger asses in a world ready to bitch slap their every foolish move. But hey, mom and dad will keep the big bad world away from hurting innocent Johnny.

Here's a news flash you big pathetic, pushover, pussy. Despite your willingness to write out checks to "fix" their mistakes, gravity may take them down anyway. So pick the time for the life lesson. Like now. Do it before their mistakes destroy your marriage, sanity, and retirement account too. Don't protect your kids from being uncomfortable or from handling things that went wrong. Let the backlash happen, and instead show them how to deal with their own dirty diapers.

Hey, you just cut the cord didn't you? Good.

<nobolz4IOU$$>

Chapter 8

Shifting Outlook

So what did we do when we finally told all of our creditors to go stick their heads in the toilet (as in paid off our debts, including our mortgage)?

We went on a vacation to our favorite coastal spot, majorly upped our monthly fun money and eat out money, and increased our monthly job evacuation plan (retirement) savings.

Here's the twisted math. Though we now work less hours and earn less money than before, we actually have more money left for fun things—because we're paying no interest on a mortgage, no interest on credit cards, no interest on student loans, no interest on car loans--nothing. Get it? Quit sucking on the bank's tits.

Being out of debt and therefore paying no interest means our lifestyle doesn't take nearly as much money. We don't need to make as much anymore. For us the answer was not earning more money. It was getting to where we needed to earn less. Do you get this, numb nuts?

We were unbelievably tempted to show off our big asses in a big rig--to buy a vanity vehicle to proclaim that we had finally arrived. Maybe hang a big set of red balls from the back hitch. But we'd be hypocrites given what I've said about wanting to look rich when you're not.

A fancy rig is just an expensive egotistical way to simply get from here to there. We just couldn't part with so much money for something that slowly rusts away. So we bought a modest and unimpressive used economy car instead. Paid cash.

Would you be okay with that? Not manly enough? Doesn't fit your image? If not, then I wonder how much you really want free from the debt ball and chain. The way I see it, while we are not driving "in style," we have more "in the bank." Without that car payment, we're a lot freer, should I lose my job. Come on dude, this isn't rocket science.

Would you rather have fancy or freedom? Ahhh, that's the kicker. Most people would truthfully rather look rich, even if the lifestyle keeps them from ever becoming rich. But our new life is not about wanting to look rich anymore. We'd rather be rich and not look it.

So what is your problem with this approach? Are you really still so hung up on your perceived image? Face it, you're probably not as beautiful or macho as you think you are. And even if you are, you should get over it, because everyone who really gets it with money thinks those who drive big fancy vanity rigs are suckers, obviously not rich either. So you're only impressing the losers anyway.

The debt free approach works. So have fun plotting what you will do when you kick the last "I owe U" in the nards! While this freedom does allow more tasty fat in your lifestyle, you'll find that your interests have shifted too and you don't always want to crave more and more like a bloated pig.

Don't get us wrong, though. Since kicking debt to the curb, it's been fun knowing that we can buy whatever we want to. Yet we still evaluate every purchase. Sometimes we say "shut the hell up" to ourselves, sometimes "go for it, ya pig!" At least now when we buy something, there is no guilt or ugly backlash later. That ups the enjoyment factor a few notches!

<nobolz4IOU$$>

Chapter 9

Because I Breathe

Somewhere along the way we have gotten an entitlement attitude, our generation. We deserve to be given credit to buy anything we want. We deserve to have a house twice as big as what our grandparents had. We need two cars, a hemi truck, and a motor home. We deserve free handouts from the government. And we deserve for our massive debt to be forgiven when we get in over our head.

If this is you, pull your fucking head out of your big, sorry, fat ass.

Here's a thought! Work hard, pay your own way, and live below your means. If you get into trouble with too much debt, pay it back, even if it means selling everything you have and starting over. Work overtime or take a second job if you have to. Don't expect the government, bank, or credit card companies to take the hit. You'll sleep better and respect the person that you see in the mirror. And the rest of us who do work their asses off won't hate you.

<nobolz4IOU$$>

Chapter 10

The Present Predicament

There's something seriously cool about giving the perfect present to someone that you love. But on the flip side, there's a good chance your gift may land in the "other than loved" category. Take that frilly fucking doily. Really, take it! So to make sure you're not just wasting time and money, here are a few ideas on gift giving.

Spend time finding out what someone likes or needs before hitting the stores. If you're not sure, then ask them or bribe someone else into asking them. Don't give a shit about the surprise factor. If you're unable to find something you know they'll want, give cash in a funny card.

Whoever said that giving cash is tacky was wrong or just wanted an excuse to hit the malls. Most people love getting cash even more than a hard on. While it may not be the most creative, crisp green paper will always be welcome. Another butt ugly tie or fairy land socks may not be!

A gift card is not the same as cash. Many people cringe at getting pre-paid gift cards. Maybe that store doesn't sell what you really want, so you have to settle for something just to use the card. How many dildos does a person really need anyway? Maybe you just don't like that store or restaurant. Maybe the last time you ate at that restaurant the waitress messed up your order and you ended up with tofu dogs on a bed of spinach. Plastic is a hassle to carry around or remember to take along….or the card expires before it's used.

Now that bites! There's just too much shit that can go wrong with gift cards—so don't curse them on others! Cash is just plain better in every way.

Stick to your budget like a fly on a steamer. If there's something just perfect, yet it is a budget buster, do not charge it. And don't eat cereal the rest of the month to pay for it. Seriously, will your friend be happy to get something that required so much sacrifice? No way! Instead divide and conquer. Get someone to join in buying the present and split the cost. You will both look brilliant in picking the perfect item, and your co-conspirator will appreciate not having to do anything more than drop by the cash machine.

If the budget is tighter than Uncle Joe's diamond making asshole, then make a gift or give coupons for providing a service, such as babysitting, house sitting, or a home-cooked meal. I'd rather get gifts like this any day.

Christmas is a customary budget buster, so set a budget and stick with it! The "love" of the season is not directly related to the amount you spend, despite everything you've seen on TV. Consider drawing names from the hat for Christmas gift exchanges, then agree on a maximum amount to spend that everyone can live with. Some people you think are rolling in money will be secretly relieved about the cost limit.

It's more fun to give kids gifts and watch their vibrant reactions. Adults don't need the gifts. Parties for adults can be boring in comparison. Most grownups have already bought everything their heart desires, so who needs presents? Booze is usually more than enough. And food. Long live rocky road chocolate cake a la mode!

Bottom line: Don't buy presents that you can't afford. And don't compare your gift to what others are giving. Style and heart are much more impressive than the price tag. And speaking of price tags, however vulgar anyone ever says it is, please include a gift receipt so it can be returned. Otherwise, don't look too closely in the back of the hall closet the next time you visit.

<nobolz4IOU$$>

Chapter 11

Miserable Miser Mending

Some people never had a spending problem…because they have always been obsessed with not spending money. They have money in the bank and still act broke. When a friend treats them to lunch, they don't return the favor. They turn down invitations to birthday parties and weddings, because buying a present is expensive. They whine that they can't afford to donate food to the shelter, because they only got a small raise this year. They jumped off the frugal train several stations back, but they are now gripping a hold bar on the selfish train.

Being tight enough to turn coal into diamonds has got to hurt somewhere! Please do not make your life all about money. It's simply a tool. The satisfaction is in the builder's hands and comes from using the tool, not merely having the tool. Let me put this in layman's terms. Having a dick is not nearly as fun as using it. The same is true for money.

But this can't be us, because we've had a problem spending too much, right? Be careful. Sometimes when people wake up from a money coma and realize that they are broke, they become obsessed with not spending any money. Along the way the carefree spender turns into the ultimate tightwad. They leap from one extreme to the other, without ever finding balance in between.

Granted, when you are drowning in debt, radical times call for a steel toe boot up the ass. It's okay (and even desirable) to flip towards the "don't spend" extreme temporarily, so that you get the ball rolling.

This could be a few months or a few years depending on your situation.

Ease up once you reach the long awaited goal, such as paying off debt, getting an emergency fund or job evacuation plan (retirement) going, or starting your kids' college fund. Or doing all of these things! Don't deprive yourself forever and turn into a miserable miser. Do something big to celebrate the major wins!

And along the way, give away some of your things, time, and money. At first this may be hard to do, but it feels so much better to give than to keep it all. If you don't give a little of your extra now, then chances are you'll never have "enough" to share.

Here are a few ideas to help you lighten up:

Make yourself spend a little on fun (there's always that adult store in the shady part of town).

Splurge on a long-desired luxury (like that house cat fur coat).

Invite a friend to join you for lunch out and pick up the tab.

Know of a family in tough times? Leave them some anonymous cash and pretend shock when you hear about the "good deed."

Do spring cleaning at your house and give the extra stuff to charity or to a friend that would use it.

Find a charity that you believe in enough to donate your time, things, or money.

Help fund a needed project at your church or in your community.

Visit a nursing home or a lonely/sick friend (sneak in some vodka).

Hand out $20 bills to strangers at Christmas.

Help provide food and shelter to people in desperate situations around in the world.

Support the local animal shelter (donate a box of twenty-two shells!).

Don't be shy about giving to people, four-legged creatures, and worthy causes. While money is tight there's always the gift of time or giving away some stuff! And helping those in tough times is the ultimate antidote for the miserable miser syndrome.

Give generously and allow yourself a few perks along the way too. Know when you have enough and are satisfied (see, that adult store item really paid off!). That's the key to truly being rich.

<nobolz4IOU$$>

Chapter 12

Rich Or Ruined?

Hey jerk off! Quit caring about looking rich.

Many of us are more concerned with looking rich than actually being rich. Think you'll get there driving a Hummer? People think being rich means having a lot of nice gear, even if it means being in debt up to our panicked eye balls.

We buy an oversized house instead of the starter house we can really afford, cheerfully sign up for sixty easy payments on furniture, lease a few of those "need something dependable" vehicles, and borrow for the got to have camper and other recreational vehicles. Then we use a credit card to "buy" the latest hi-tech gadgets to entertain us along the way. Life is a ball! Too bad the ball is attached to a chain.

Either that ball has knocked us senseless, or the chain is cutting off oxygen to our brain, because we're acting like we're addicted to crack.

We now have to work, work, work to pay the "I.O.U.'s." For many of us, if we lose a job, then we can lose everything. We're living from paycheck to paycheck. This is the stupidest way to live. Before you say, "A lot of people can't help it that they're struggling with money," let me say, yes, you are correct. But most people are living paycheck to paycheck because they can't say no to the spoiled brat that lives inside of them: "But I want it! I really want it! I have to have it now!"

You know what you need to tell that obnoxious kid inside of you? "Too fucking bad, you're not getting it." If you can't do that, then you might as well shove this book in by the toilet paper dispenser and use it to wipe your sorry ass over the next week or so, because that's about all the good it will do you.

Many Europeans only work about thirty hours per week. So why do people in the United States work so much? Usually it's because of our long "wish list"…and the resulting "debt list." We can't tell ourselves no.

The worst part about having to work so much is that many of us are in this position voluntarily! We're doing this simply because we are buying too much horse shit and borrowing too much money. So we're stuck in jobs with sucky bosses, working longer hours than we want to. Then, we use up too much of our remaining free time to take care of all our stuff. Oh, we are so rich, aren't we!

Being rich isn't about having the most things, the fanciest things, or even largest bank balance. Being rich is having the choice of how to spend your time. The more stuff and debt you have, the less control you have over how you spend your time. Brilliant, huh!

<nobolz4IOU$$>

Chapter 13

Piranha Plastic

We've been lied to about paying with plastic. Receiving that "elite" card doesn't mean we've arrived. It doesn't make our lives any easier or better. And it wasn't sent in the mail to benefit us. Pull your plastic head out of your ass.

Because people have more heartburn handing over cash, the banks and credit card companies send plastic cards so we'll spend more. Thoughtful of them, huh? Freaking bastards. It's hard to know what people buy when they use cash, so credit cards also help them track our buying habits. Then an ad for the perfect thing just happens to arrive in the mail…

Plastic doesn't help us (the consumer) in any tangible way. It's just created more headaches. Just ask the person trying to get their money back after someone stole their debit card. Or ask the person who is out of control with credit card debt.

But unfortunately plastic is probably here to stay, so here are a few rules to guide you.

Plastic Rule #1 – Do not carry a balance

If you can't pay off the credit card balance within thirty days, then you shouldn't have any credit cards. None. This sounds harsh, but friends need to tell each other the truth. The interest rates listed on the bills are probably scarier than some roller coasters. And a lot less fun. Close all of the credit card accounts and pay them off. Then stick with cash until the self-control fairy visits your home.

If you have no credit card debt or routinely pay off credit card balances every month, then congratulations! Give yourself a hand job. When you come down off your high horse, make sure there are no annual fees and that they don't pull tricks like the beastly brats that live next door. If a card company starts getting greedy, then dump them like last night's burnt dinner. There's plenty of competition for your business and you can do better than them.

Plastic Rule #2 – Use a credit card for risky purchases

Use your credit card for any transaction that is risky, such as online or over the phone purchases, hotel and car reservations, and any time you get a bad vibe. Why? If a card number gets stolen, it's better for the credit card company to be out the money then your checking account. Hey, maybe there is something good about plastic…

Plastic Rule #3 – Pay cash as much as possible for everything

You will spend less when the bill is paid with some "presidents" from your wallet. Using a check, debit card or credit card doesn't affect your hands or mind the same way.

Still, sometimes it's not possible to pay with cash, so use a check or debit card before pulling out a credit card. There is one word of caution. Some businesses, such as hotels and gas stations, put a temporary hold on some of your funds as soon as you swipe your debit card. Pay these things with cash, or keep a cushion in your bank account to ensure your account is never overdrawn from holds.

Handing over greenbacks is also impressive, fun, and glam. And a bit of a novelty these days…bet people will take notice. Plus, you can annoy people behind you in the checkout lines to no end by always digging out exact change.

<nobolz4IOU$$>

Chapter 14

Bank On It

Appreciate my pet peeves about the lending institutions I just love to hate.

Pay Day Loan Stores:

At the top of the list, those annoying payday loan stores should be run out of town with pitchforks shoved up their asses by an angry mob. These pesky "shark" stores are helping to drown you and the poorest of your neighbors. The average 20% annual interest rate on credit cards looks like a great deal next to the shark store's 200% per month interest rate.

Don't believe the payday advance stores charge that high a rate? Then you may want to sit down before you check the fine print on the contract. The only thing that's inflated here is their profit margin, and your stupid gland if you use them. They have figured out how to shift your wealth to them and apparently people are more than okay with that.

Credit Card Companies:

Credit cards have their place as a temporary method of payment, but not for carrying a balance and certainly not to pay for every transaction.

How many of us play the credit card "bonus award" games? Do not fall for any of their marketing schemes. Their game rules were designed so you pick up the tab (by carrying a balance) and they make a tidy profit when life happens and you can't pay the balance off as you originally planned and instead have to make the minimum payments. It's an idiot lotto. Don't play it. You don't need their freaking hats and trinkets and points for nothing.

Don't be a dick. Life is going to happen, so prepare for it by having a cash fund. If you can't pay cash for something, don't charge it and don't buy it. If you do and your credit card picks up the slack, then expect to pay premium for the "help." Just don't cry like a little school girl because you're a broke scallywag.

Banks:

Banking establishments have lots of ways to sting you with fees. In fact, they've become masters at it. And the range and size of the various fees has gotten absurd. If your bank doesn't offer a free checking account, then change banks or join a local credit union.

Do not get overdraft protection on your checking account--instead have the charges declined. If the funds aren't available, then you can't afford it, you little whiner. It's by far more comfortable to have a store clerk deny you a purchase, then to have no money to pay for minor things like heat, rent, and food.

So learn to balance a check book and do not bounce checks. After all, don't you have something better to do with your hard-earned paycheck than to pay bank fees? They're banking that you don't.

<nobolz4IOU$$>

Chapter 15

Compound Me Negative, Baby!

I know a sure-fire way to get a 20% annual interest rate—open a credit card and charge it up!

Many people plot and ponder ways to increase the return on their savings and investments. Few think about "negative compounding" as the other clever way to get some "high returns." Negative compounding is simply "you paying you" by not giving it away to others. It's an idiotically simple concept.

Pay off the credit cards. Get a 20% return or more immediately! Who knew?! Paying only the minimum amount due on a credit card is a moron tax on people who don't know or care that the item will cost double by the time it's paid off. Da! Why do you think they set the minimum payments so low? Think twice before plunking down the plastic.

Pay off student loans. They won't go away even in a bankruptcy, so tackle them early in the game. Don't defer them either or they'll grow like your girlfriend's nasty yeast infection. Ah, right, your ex-girlfriend who kept, err, ah, deferring to do anything about it. Student loans shouldn't be hanging around long enough to see your grandkids born.

Pay off other loans and debts. It doesn't really matter if you pay off those with the highest balance or highest interest rate first. You're going to knock them all out soon anyway. Choose the strategy that gives you the biggest hard on. Then pick the first target and go at it like a Chihuahua going after your Uncle Charlie's leg. And don't stop there. Move on to the cat, and the neighbor's Pomeranian too...keep going until you are an undefeated stud.

Quit borrowing money, period. Always pay with cash, check, or debit card. If you don't have cash, then you can't afford it. Only use a credit card as a method of payment if you can pay it off within 30 days. No bellyaching.

Save HUGE by not buying stuff. While you can't always purchase what you want, you can probably rent it by the hour like an over-the-hill hooker, borrow it for a week like your neighbor's unwanted dog doo in your yard, or do without it forever like a nasty case of crabs!

The returns from "negative compounding" are significant. With focus, many people pay off everything (except the house) within one to two years. So how focused are you to shake off the debt, much like Uncle Charlie shook off that little teacup mutt into the fire pit?

<nobolz4IOU$$>

Chapter 16

Fanatics Wanted

Most people prefer to stay with familiar problems, rather than find solutions that may create brief havoc in their life. This is nuttier than you and your gonads jumping in an icy lake. If your feet outgrew your shoes, then you'd replace the shoes, even if the new pair felt stiff and uncomfortable for a bit. Right?

There was something to be said for the old hot wire up the pee pee to cure what ailed the shore leaved sailor. But nowadays people are so squeamish over any treatment that may be painful. No pain, no gain.

Maybe it's time to consider:

- Renting for a while longer, instead of buying a house.
- Selling the house and renting instead.
- Moving to a less expensive area.
- Selling the house and buying a smaller house.
- Selling a car that has a loan balance, paying off the upside portion and buying an older vehicle with cash.
- Selling the big rig and getting a smaller one.
- Selling the boat.
- Selling the camper.
- Buying used stuff instead of buying it new.
- Renting stuff instead of buying it (campers, boats, tools).
- Selling anything you don't use or need.
- Selling everything and starting over!!!

Would you be willing to do ANY of the above, if that's what it took? Or does the idea make you cringe like the thought of having a red hot metal wire shoved up the you know what?

You can always buy things later when you are no longer struggling. Yes, it can be very hard to let go of stuff. Still, once you start doing it, it becomes very liberating. I should know. At the height of our money troubles, my wife and I sold the house and most everything else too.

We sold a newer car at a loss, even though it cost us several thousand dollars to pay off the auto loan. Ouch! We bought a cheap, older car for cash. We lived in a small basement apartment. Doing these things put us in a position to get out of debt much faster and took a lot of the pressure off. If we had insisted on keeping all of the junk, it would have cost even more in the end and taken us longer to get out of debt.

Do we have stuff today? Yes, some nice things, even though we still tend to keep things simple and downsized. But we can and do splurge sometimes…because with no debt we can afford to do pretty much whatever we want. And now we're the one who owns the bling, not the bank!

<nobolz4IOU$$>

Chapter 17

Rags To Radical

I'll always remember exactly where I was driving nine years ago when the light bulb went on that I'd totally screwed up with money in nearly every way. What a jerk! My relationship with money needed to change, and before the wedding in a month, or else it would affect my marriage more than some old girlfriend showing up at the house pregnant.

So as soon as we got married, we got radical and clawed our way out of the debt that I brought into the marriage. It took months and months of working overtime, commuting three hours a day, living in a rented basement apartment, and driving old cars. Was it an inconvenience? Fuck yes.

We put every spare dime into paying off debt. We didn't blow money on all the "fun" things that we watched our family and friends do. But the results were huge – two years later all of the I.O.U's were paid off.

Can you imagine what it feels like to have absolutely no debt!? It feels so damn good, and worth every bit of work and sacrifice to get there. Being debt free opens a lot of doors.

A month after we paid off the debt, I got laid off…and we went out to dinner to celebrate. Now I was forced to look for a job closer to home and quit the commuting. We easily lived off of my wife's income as a secretary, without tapping into our skimpy emergency savings. While we weren't too worried about the situation, it was nice when another job came along. We kept living "the undersized life," and plunked the extra into our savings.

Two years later we put a 40% down payment on a brand new house. Four years after buying our house, living the same frugal way we had lived while we got out of deft, it was completely paid off.

Now imagine what you can do with no debt and a paid off house! Do you think life is a little sweeter? Hell yea! Without a mortgage payment, we can work any jobs we want and work fewer hours. We can buy whatever we want (yet things don't turn our crank as much these days). We can do whatever we want to. We have more spare time. We are rich and we aren't even millionaires (yet!).

No one handed us an easy way out of our financial mess. We decided to kick our own asses into submission. We learned to tell our cash where to go and changed our spending habits.

Now just imagine if we had learned these things earlier in life. We'd be really rich in money and time. But we were late financial bloomers – just like many of you. You can do this too.

<nobolz4IOU$$>

Chapter 18

You Blooming Consumer

Whoever came up with the term "consumer" anyway? Do we devour, use up, waste, and squander? Most people do this quite often, thoroughly, and without thinking. And that's the problem. When it comes to blowing our wads like there's no tomorrow, we're like dogs returning to our own pools of vomit.

The meaning of the word isn't important unless it reflects your actions. So…do you often leave the store with more than you planned to buy? Got an impressive number of toys, too?

Being a compulsive spender is good for the bank. It's good for the credit card company. And yes, it's even pretty good for the government. It's good for everyone but you.

So why are you acting like you care more about the establishment than yourself? Why do you think it's okay to make everyone else rich? Pull your head out of your big rear end! If you spend every dollar of your paycheck, then you're giving away your wealth.

Definition of Consumer: A freaking idiot who spends all they make on things, saves very little money, if any, and willingly works far harder and longer than they would have to because they love making the banks, credit card companies, and government richer.

<nobolz4IOU$$>

Chapter 19

Accidental Probability

My method of winning with money is not about luck or probabilities. Playing the lotto every day, when you hit the stop-and-rob quickie mart to buy three tall boys and a pack of smokes like a loser, is not my idea of a retirement plan. Nor do I think a trip to Vegas to going to prosper anyone's life except the casinos and escort services.

The method for winning with money is pretty certain. In fact, it's so boring that most people yawn themselves into a coma before they even get started. You don't have to be in the right place at the right time. You just have to do a few simple things consistently:

Keep track of where your money goes.
Live on less than what you make.
Quit borrowing money.
Pay off all debt.
Save.

Anyone who applies these strategies like they're prison meat if they don't, can quickly get out of the poor house and onto easy street. This method is time-tested and proven. It works every time. But you, you keep dropping the soap in the shower! That would explain your life with money too—you must like getting corn holed.

<nobolz4IOU$$>

Chapter 20

Muscle Bound

Most of us started building our financial muscles later than we should have. If you spent a fraction of the time you played with the muscle between your legs, as you did developing your financial muscles, well, you wouldn't be reading this book. But here you are. So get mad about being a financial pussy and do something about it!

Think of someone that has it all together. Finances, family, free time—a whole balanced life. Unless their wealth was inherited, their "good luck" was not an accident. They worked their ass off and sacrificed things, things that others consider requirements, in order to be where they are today.

Chances are that five years ago you would have considered this same person a schmuck for denying themselves some nice things, so they could be ahead in the future. Well the future has arrived. And now you long to be that financially "ripped" schmuck, don't you?

So it's time to get going. If not, you will regret letting another block of time go to waste when you wake up and suddenly find you're still as broke as your dick's erectile dysfunction.

Here is your "to-do" list, in the order that you should do them:

Do a budget every month (and keep doing it when you get out of this mess, so you don't get back into this mess).

While you're getting out of debt, have at least $500 to $1,000 in an emergency fund at all times.

Get completely out of debt (except the house).

After the debt is paid off, increase your emergency fund to eight to twelve months of living expenses.

Save big in retirement and investments (5% to 20% of your income).

If you have kids, contribute monthly to a college saving account.

Pay off the house (while continuing to save for retirement, investments, and college).

After the house is paid off, save even bigger for retirement, investments, and college.

You'll have to do some research to put "numbers" to many of these things, like how much you should be saving for your job evacuation plan (retirement). That's just part of the planning process. It's not fun to do this stuff. I don't enjoy it at all. But I enjoy being broke much less.

Here's a bonus to help take some of the tedium from the climb out of the hole. Don't forget to give along the way to charities and causes that set you on fire. Do this during all of the steps, in proportion to what you can afford at the time.

<nobolz4IOU$$>

Chapter 21

Simple Numbers

Tell your money where it will go, or like a naughty child, it will go somewhere else and do what you don't want it to do—likely at the most embarrassing times.

This is the toughest, most dull and tedious, yet greatest topic to cover with your money. The big bitchy budget. Don't skim over this section.

Creating a budget is the key to your financial orgasm. Don't be scared of tackling a little piece of paper every month. It's not rocket science. Like a brilliantly executed football game, a budget is a game plan on how to spend the money before you begin the play. Without careful planning, even the best team will have dismal results on the field.

You don't need a fancy ass computer program to do budgeting. In fact, unless you're a freaking geek who loves analyzing things down to the tiniest detail, don't waste your money on elaborate software. Of course, if you were that kind of geek, you probably wouldn't need this book in the first place. Or, if you are that geek, you may have trouble seeing the forest for the trees. Either way, read on.

While I like to use an Excel spreadsheet, any word processing program, or even a hand-written version would work just as well. Regardless of how you "write it down," after a few months it should get to where this process only take ten to fifteen minutes per month. If it takes longer, then you are making this too complex. Keep it simple, like your choices in what underwear to put on every morning, or you won't stick with it.

At the beginning of each month, list your income in one column and your expenses in another column. Look at the last few bank statements to make a list of the spending categories, and then figure out how much you actually spent each month on clothing, entertainment, etc. Brace yourself.

It will be a shock to find out how much more you spend on groceries and eating out than you realized....and alarming to realize how much money just evaporated. Stuffing your face is probably one of the biggest expenses you have and chances are, if you're like most of America, it shows.

Once you can breathe again, figure out how much you want to spend in each category. What you used to spend on something is not what you must continue to spend on it. You are in control now (use your mind— the rational part, not your heart or your feelings or your stomach).

A budget lists what you always spend money on and other things, even if they don't come up every month. A typical list may include:

Babysitting, birthdays, booze, cable TV, car maintenance, car tabs, cell phone, Christmas, clothes, college fund, credit cards, dates, eating out, electricity, emergency fund, entertainment, fun money (you're going to blow money anyway, so list it), gas for cars, gifts, giving to charity, groceries, haircuts, home decorating, home maintenance, house cleaning, insurance (car, home, life, medical), internet, loans (car, student loans, etc), natural gas, prescriptions and co-pays, phone, property tax, rent/mortgage, retirement funds, savings, school expenses, sex supplies (just checking whether you're reading or skimming),vacations, water/sewer/garbage.

List everything. If you forget something, add it the first time it comes for a surprise visit, like smelly Aunt Urma. While figuring out your list accurately may be tedious and painful, a budget is the key to avoiding a heap of more painful things.

Once you have these two lists (income and expenses) written down, total up each one. There has to be enough income to cover the expenses. Adjust the amounts of your expenses until the total equals your income…not less and not more. And if expenses are less than income—woohoo! Solve this "problem" by increasing your savings. If you are married, this is where you discuss and plan together. This is also a chance to learn about your spouse's dreams, which usually require some cash to achieve.

Try to stick to what you put on paper as close as you can. Before making a purchase, ask yourself "is it in the budget?" If the answer is "no," then something in the budget needs to go down by the same amount, so you don't spend more money than you have. That's how it works. If surprise expenses keep showing up, then maybe a new line needs to be added to the budget. (If you are married, it's time for a group huddle.)

Remember not to charge anything that you cannot immediately pay off. That includes vacations. Budget for your vacation and don't splurge more than that amount. Spending money that you do not have is a guaranteed road to poverty, not to relaxation.

A tip for singles: A budget will help you reach your goals. Yet it's easy to blow it without accountability. Consider asking a friend to give you some tough words when they are needed.

A tip for married couples: It's okay to change the budget mid-month, as long as you both agree to it. Of course, if something new drives the budget up, then something else has to be reduced. Promise not to vary from the budget unless you both agree ahead of time. Keeping that promise will build your trust in each other, and relax fears that there won't be enough greenbacks to carry you through the month.

Budgets seem unromantic, yet it gets everyone to reveal their dreams and priorities in order to create a plan that will take you where you want to go. Being this candid with each other can save your sanity and marriage.

And blowing the plan without the other spouse's agreement is a big, big deal. Don't do it. Nothing is worth losing your spouse's trust. If someone keeps sabotaging the plan, then consider marriage counseling because there's more than a money difference going on. Seriously.

Two things help my wife and I keep track of the budget during the month. First, we print out the budget and carry it everywhere, marking things off as we spend the money. Second, to help us not overspend in our areas of weakness, we carry cash in envelopes for groceries, eating out, and fun money. When the money in the "eat out" envelope is gone, then we have to stop eating out until the next month. That goes the same for the other cash envelopes too.

Want more tips on doing a budget? Simply do a search on the internet for sample budget forms and advice from experts. Or go down to the public library and look for books on the subject. Whatever approach you decide on, remember that simple works best.

It may take several months of wrestling with the budget before you get it right. Don't give up! It is worth it. Remember you didn't learn how to drive a car on the first attempt. And you wouldn't consider driving anywhere without knowing where you want to go and figuring out how to get there. Your first date was probably a joke too and now you're a seasoned pro. Everything worthwhile takes some time and effort. Don't give up.

Remember that your money has no more self-control than you do. Make sure you both behave.

You worked your ass off to earn the money. Put the same effort into keeping it!

<nobolz4IOU$$>

Chapter 22

The Throwaways

Chances are you blow 20% to 40% of your paycheck on fluff (wants, not needs). Then you have the nerve to complain about not having anything left to save for your job evacuation plan (retirement), pay off the nagging debts, or build an emergency fund. What a whiny little girl!

While you seem to be "getting by" to your friends and others in your family, in reality you are not going anywhere and the boat is slowly sinking, one drop of water at a time! Remember, every dollar you piss away on these things now will have to be re-earned before you can ever quit having to work. Do you want to work forever, ya numbskull?

Take a brutal look at what you actually spend all of your money on every month. That means adding it up, then targeting where you can cut out some fat. And I can guarantee you, there is a lot of fat. Your spending needs a liposuction. And here's the direct benefit: Instead of sinking the boat you can build a huge retirement or savings account one drop at a time by plugging some of these seemingly small money leaks.

Think this is easy? Okay, Einstein, let's see if you can do without some of these perks.

Can you do without buying lunch out most days (packing a lunch requires getting up five minutes earlier…hmm…that is looking like an expensive five minute luxury)?

Can you do without eating dinner out as much as you do (you could have a freezer full of your homemade, single-serving leftovers to eat on those exhausting days)?

Can you do without expensive coffee at the local coffee grinder shop (you can make your own so cheap and easy)?

Can you do without buying more toys for the kids (that they probably won't play with) whenever you feel guilty about being away from them so often?

Can you do without the super deluxe cable or satellite television package?

Can you do without buying things that are simply "impulse" candy? Like more clothes when your closet is already full.

Can you do without cell phones for you, spouse, each kid, plus the dog and cat?

Can you do without constantly "upgrading" your electronic gadgets with the very latest technology (when there's absolutely nothing wrong with what you already have)?

Can you do without buying everything new and top of the line?

Can you do without going to the movie theatre for every new movie, rather than waiting until the release hits the rental store? If you do go to the movies, definitely cut out buying the snack extortions there.

Can you do without buying things that you rarely use (rather than renting or borrowing)?

Can you do without telling the kids or spouse or yourself "yes," even though your wallet is shouting "no?"

Can you do without driving yourself to work, rather than carpooling or using the bus?

Can you do without caving in to friends/family to do or buy something, even when it doesn't sound like fun or you can't afford it?

Can you do without driving the gas hog rig, rather than a boring economy car?

Don't know where to start? Find a stick of dynamite, hold it between your legs and light the fuse—you'll think of something quick! If your situation is frantic, then every single splurge may need to get cut out until the pressure eases. It may suck to be you for a while—you're probably used to that. But your future will look a lot brighter when you stop dumping it on worthless stuff.

<nobolz4IOU$$>

Chapter 23

Don't Label Me

Does the word "frugal" bring up a picture of some sweater-wearing, milk toast, mamby pamby, stingy, unmarried, unkempt, uncouth miser with a stick up his rear end? This character mainly eats those bargain brand TV dinners and generic macaroni and cheese, right? He gives gifts of last year's recycled fruit cake. His mattresses and floorboards are bulging with cash, yet he avoids spending it at all costs.

Nobody wants to be that miserably stingy. So instead we strive for that "broke yet splurging anyway" dick-on-our-forehead Hummer mentality, forgetting that there is a middle ground between these two extremes.

Frugal is not a four-letter word for "tightwad." Get it through your think skull. It's really the neighbor who lives across the street in a modest-sized house that was paid for long ago, has well over a million in investments and job evacuation plan (retirement) accounts, doesn't have to work anymore at age fifty-seven, spends his time doing fun hobbies (some of which make money), takes his family on trips all the time, gives generously to charities, enjoys life to the fullest, and doesn't stress over money at all! That is frugal at its best. The mega-planner who gets things done! Be that.

Put some FRUGAL "style" into your bean curd:

Fun
Relaxed
Unrestrained
Generous
Alive
Laughing - all the way to the frickin' bank.

<nobolz4IOU$$>

Chapter 24

Get Some Taste

Groceries tend to be one of the larger monthly expenses. With varying success, we have tried different approaches to keep the cost under control. While many people rave about couponing, my wife and I thought it required too much effort for too little savings. Plus it drove us nuts, not to mention that most of what coupons are good for is processed shit that you shouldn't even feed your dog. No wonder America is fat and unhealthy.

Not to worry. There are other ways to save money and time without the migraine factor. Ever hear of Russian Roulette? Oops—don't want to give away the book ending.

Try the envelope system. My wife and I use this method for any expense that tends to get out of control, such as groceries, eating out, entertainment, and fun money. Here's how it works. Decide how much to spend on groceries, place the money inside an envelope, and then use only that money to buy groceries. Now here's the hard part—when the envelope is empty, stop buying. Until the next month's budget rolls around, live off the food that's sitting in your pantry. Don't be a puss and cheat.

Stockpile when your favorite foods and the basics are on sale and build your meals around those foods. The more food that is sitting in your pantry, the less often you have to go grocery shopping. Bet you won't cry like a school girl about having some time freed up by using this strategy!

Skip grocery shopping one weekend a month and live off the pantry or freezer offerings. This frees up cash and time. Plus it gets you to eat food that's been pushed into the back of your pantry and freezer that's nearing the expiration date. Or at least you can find all the hidden spore-ridden packages and burn them. Sometimes shopping smart means not shopping at all.

Only buy fruit and vegetables that are in season locally. This is not just a cost issue. Off-season, shipped-in produce tastes like glue, because it was picked before it was ripe to survive the shipping process. Sometimes it's artificially colored or treated to look ripe. Yuck! Fuck! That sucks!

Create a shopping list (so you won't be prone to impulse) and stick with it. A mission without a plan, like your desire to strike it rich from the lotto, fails.

Don't buy prepared meals at the grocery store. They're designed to kill you while making someone else richer. No shit. Instead, cook a double portion (or larger) for dinner and freeze the extra in single serving containers. On the days when you come home exhausted, you'll be eternally grateful to find home-cooked lasagna sitting in the freezer waiting for you. And it will taste amazing, be healthier, and cheaper than "production line" meals.

Don't buy snacks that you can make yourself. They're designed to kill you and make someone else rich. A homemade version is better tasting, healthier, and cheaper.

This is key, lard ass! Nothing beats the quality of garden fresh foods. Eat all the fresh produce you can, then freeze and preserve some too. Consider planting a garden and enjoy watching it grow. Even if gardening doesn't turn your crank, I bet you know people that do (garden, that is). While my wife and I don't have a garden, we sure love it when friends give us tomatoes from their garden!

Or shop at the local Farmer's Market—you'll find high-quality, fresh fruits and vegetables. Sometimes local quality food costs a bit more, but your body and taste buds will thank you. Plus eating right can help you stay healthy and avoid costly medical expenses down the road.

<nobolz4IOU$$>

Chapter 25

Losing The Losers

When you start rebuilding your life, someone will rain on your parade. So always carry an umbrella, a sense of humor, and a pair of numb chucks!

"Energy Drainers" will tell you that it can't be done....even if you just did it. Some of your strongest critics will come disguised as close family and friends. People that you knew were on your side. Stunned, you will wonder why they aren't encouraging or happy for you. These cloud makers will also have a long list of reasons why they couldn't possibly do the same thing and why you were somehow luckier.

Chances are they need to make similar changes, but are not ready to make them. That's okay, because yesterday you weren't ready either. Give them space. Their mind-set has nothing to do with you reaching the goal. Don't bother arguing; simply change the subject.

If your friends won't drop the pity pot attitude, then drop them faster than the hot lump of charcoal thrown at you by your drunken cousin during a beer bash. It's better to have one unfailing ally than a bunch of "sort-of" comrades.

And if you wouldn't take that attitude from a friend, then do not take it from family either. Having a DNA link does not excuse someone for acting ugly. Don't put up with crap from your family.

A sure way to annoy Energy Drainers is to cheerfully point out how screwed up their life is and tactlessly declare how it can be fixed. That will give them a nice big cup of shut the fuck up. Yes, there are times when it's fun to torment those aggravating downers. The key is not to mess with people you like.

When people want your advice, they will ask for it. Until then there's an endless list of "other" things to talk about, like last night's football game and how many beers you downed during halftime.

P.S. Don't ask your broke friends and family for money advice. And if they offer any advice, do not follow it. Well, you can follow it if you really want to….just expect to end up broker.

<nobolz4IOU$$>

Chapter 26

Exercising Relationships

Okay couch potato. Listen up or I'll have to crack a yard stick across your knuckles faster a nun who's had enough of a student's sniveling.

Take care of your body if you want to improve your quality of life now, and especially when you're older. Health problems are expensive and a bitch to deal with. One of the keys to good health, in addition to eating the right foods, is a regular exercise routine.

The best exercise routine is one you can do with someone else like your spouse, a friend, your kids, a parent, or a brother or sister. Walking, running, biking, hiking, tennis, swimming—they're all good. You can build relationships and tone your muscles at the same time. Plus, you're more likely to get some exercise if one of you is always nagging the other to do it.

My wife and I love to walk and bike ride. The forty-five minute to one hour walks are especially good talking time. We find excuses to walk—like to the library, downtown, to the store, or that ally behind the bar where we can dig wine bottles out of the garbage for making lights.

Walking got us hooked because it gave us the chance to de-stress while we talked about our day, our dreams, job stresses, family, and money. Many financial achievements have been planned thanks to these daily walks. We strategized about getting out of debt and paying off the house on our walks. Walking that last mortgage payment a half mile to the mail box was a very liberating moment we will never forget.

Walking with the jogging stroller also kept our baby daughter content and quiet—that stroller got a lot a miles put on it when she was little. The miles just floated by. We'd arrive home stoked from the endorphins too. And we've stayed trim as a result. We've read that married couples put on a few pounds every year. Not us.

Without question our marriage is better for doing this "exercise."

Make time in your busy schedule for strength building and relationship building together. No amount of money can substitute for good health and improved relationships with family and friends.

<nobolz4IOU$$>

Chapter 27

Uncle Herb Wants Out

The fastest way to fuck up a relationship with family or friends is to mix money into the equation. Don't do it! Get-togethers with family and friends will never feel the same again. You probably won't feel quite as grateful during those Thanksgiving dinners if you owe money or are owed money. No matter how good Aunt Sue's turkey is, it just won't be the same when your cousin Lester owes you five hundred big ones.

Invest your time, heart, and soul in your family and friends. But do not add money to the mixture, or it will taste like your niece's first attempt at cooking, or squirrel poop.

Usually family or friends go into business together when one or both parties are too broke to do it alone. Why this isn't a huge red flag with "screw me now or later" scrolled across it is beyond reason. The plan is doomed to end in regret. What happens when Uncle Herb needs out and the others can't afford to buy him out?

The reality is, people retire, kids head off to college, health and financial issues often come up without warning. If someone really needs to get out of the deal, yet the other party doesn't have the funds to buy them out, then resentment will start eating away at those feeling like they've been shafted.

Buying a vacation home together is a much safer adventure, right? The logic goes, hotels are expensive so let's get all the siblings to buy a vacation home together and share the costs—then everyone will save on vacations. Horse shit. Stupid. Huge red flag. What will happen to the place and your relationships when Beth can't pay her part of the mortgage or her portion of the new roof? You'll have to write out a bigger check to cover the difference, or watch the "retreat" go into neglect. What if your boneheaded brother Billy can't pay his part of the expenses to you? Vacations will never feel the same again.

Never co-sign a loan or give a personal loan to anyone. That includes loans for a home, business, car, student loan, credit card, appliances, or anything. If the bank won't give your bum son a loan on his own, then he isn't likely to pay up. If you co-sign on the loan, then you'd better plan on being the one to pay it back...and to never get reimbursed. And worst of all, your relationship will be forever affected over something that they couldn't afford and shouldn't have bought in the first place. Have some tough love, man!

If you can afford to help out a family member truly in need (again, try to differentiate between their want and their need), then give them the money without any strings attached to it. Gifts are fine (as long as they're not bail-outs), co-signing for loans is not.

<nobolz4IOU$$>

Chapter 28

Married Money

Money and relationships only go together if two people are married. Otherwise finances should be kept separate.

Once you say "I do," then invest in your spouse and share the whole money thing. If you don't share the money planning together, then how together are you, really?

Keep talking, listening, and compromising until you both agree on how the money is to be spent. This is a more intimate discussion than most people anticipate. There may even be some fighting. And if you're fighting about how to spend the money, understand this: It is because some of your basic life values are not in alignment. This is serious. You'd better come to an agreement or your marriage may hit the fan like ape shit.

Regardless of who brings home the largest paycheck, every spouse has an equal say at this bargaining table. Stay-at-home spouses are never off the clock, and get full rights to everything. Get it, meat head (husband)? Don't belittle your wife because she makes less than you or stays home with the kids. She has every bit as much right to decide how the money is spent as you do. Don't be a big schlong about it.

Excluding any amount budgeted for each person's "fun money," give your word to each other that you will not make a purchase, or change the budget, without both being in agreement. If either party is not on board, then the ship does not sail forward! If someone keeps sailing the ship alone to buy more cargo, then marriage counseling may be on the horizon. Or a cannon ball upside the spleen.

Listen to each other. Women often have "gut" feelings that are uncanny. If you ignore her "bad vibe" or "I don't have a good felling" about something, later you'll probably find out what that warning was about after you lose your shirt. On the flipside, men tend to have an easier time taking emotion out of the equation. Listen to his reasoning, girls. He may be a big Neanderthal, but every once in a while he's right. Hunches and logic are both essential, and neither is more important than the other.

Bottom line, don't buy if either person has a hesitation—it's just not worth sabotaging your spouse's trust over some ridiculous junk.

<nobolz4IOU$$>

Chapter 29

Worthless Money

Although I bitch and moan a lot about money in this book, life is not ultimately about money. Having enough investments to justify hiring a personal investment adviser does not mean that someone has "arrived." That's just not the case. There are plenty of unfulfilled millionaires in the world. A life without purpose is not improved with money.

A banker once approached the owner of a small bakery about "improving" the business. His fresh baked breads were amazing. With good credit he could borrow and establish a franchise. Then he could have it all—a custom house, flashier car, and a jaw-dropping income. Eventually the baker could sell the bakery franchise, retire, and then do whatever he liked.

The baker just shook his head and replied, "I already love what I do. At noon on Tuesdays through Saturdays, I'm done working. Every Sunday and Monday, I'm off. Expanding the business would require working more days and hours, so when would I find time for what's important? If anything, I'm going to cut back even more on work hours, since my kids will be grown soon and I promised the wife that we'd travel more. I don't love money as much as I do time with my family."

Money is only a handy tool to help you live your dreams. No matter your net worth, only when you're living your dream will you have a truly rich life.

<nobolz4IOU$$>

Chapter 30

Short Challenges

No one ever thinks "I can't wait to turn my kid into a spoiled brat!" Yet somehow that bundle of joy turns into a mouthy two-legged kid with an entitled attitude. It happens easily and with the best of intentions. No good deed goes unpunished.

We remember going without as a child, then decide that our child is NOT going to miss out too. So we give them everything….even stuff they don't want, like, or need!

Absurdly, stuff doesn't satisfy. So it's never enough. Welcome little diva and little monster! Little fuck and little shit, is more like it. Later we wonder why Jessica or Johnnie don't do anything for themselves (let alone around the house to help out), and we are irritated about being taken for granted. It's your own damn fault, mom and dad, for coddling the little bastard.

Give your kids love—lots of it—but don't give them everything they want. Give your kids the gift of getting less, so they learn creativity and determination. This builds their character while maintaining your bank account balance. How cool is that? A priceless lesson that is free! But the question is: Do you have the balls to do it?

Do away with an allowance. Handing your kids money that they did not earn isn't doing them a freaking favor. The real world does not work that way. Try skipping work and see if there's a check (or a job) waiting for you on payday. No way!

Teach your kids a work ethic by putting them on straight commission. Even a three year old, with help and praise, can pick up their toys. Create a list of tasks for your kids to complete, and then do not pay them until the work is done. If you think this is too much of a hard ass approach, and you don't mind your kids robbing you for the rest of your life, then go ahead and skip to the next chapter, ya little Nancy.

Make sure your kid puts something into savings and gives some away to a needy cause. And make sure it's their money, not yours, that's sitting on the table. Sometimes we try to teach our kids how to give by giving to them. Spoiler alert—this is only teaching them how to take. They won't learn to give by passing out money that you gave to them. They'll just learn to have their little grubby paws outstretched for a handout.

The only way to learn generosity is by giving away something you've earned. Once these habits are deep-rooted, they are there for life. If you don't teach them this with some real tenacity, they'll just turn into another broke citizen, always looking for government handouts and bailouts.

Within limits, let them decide what to buy with their newly earned wealth. It is better for them to have things of their own taste, than a room full of shiny shit they won't play with.

And when the money runs out, do not "help" them out with their next purchase. Money usually runs out before the wish list does, so let your kids learn some patience and judgment. Do not become their personal Parent Savings and Loan.

When they're older and want to buy bigger things (like a car) then consider matching their savings as an incentive for them to save. Here's one note of caution.

Do not treat your match as a bartering tool for future "good" behavior. If they save, you match.

While you are having fun teaching your kid about real life, you might find the kid inside you again.

<nobolz4IOU$$>

Chapter 31

Rude Investment Or Mannerly Manor?

Is a house really a great investment? Ooh, I love this one because most people get it all wrong.

If the home was purchased with cash, then it may provide a somewhat stable investment. If you have a mortgage, then the answer is probably "no," it bites as an investment. Having a mortgage payment really changes the math.

Now don't get me wrong, owning a house can be a really good thing, especially after the intangible benefits are considered, such as raising a family in it. But too many people assume that buying a house is automatically a great investment. It's not necessarily-- especially if you borrow the money. I shouldn't need to rehash the 2008 shit that hit the fan.

Add up the cost of buying and owning a house. For example, if you financed the majority of your house, it may add up something like this: Mortgage interest at 4% + property tax at 1% + maintenance at 2% + inflation at 3% = 10% grand total.

Yes geeks, this is extremely simplified but it's only to make a point. If your house is not going up in value by 10% per year, then you are losing money on your "great investment."

Of course, the math looks better than a tarred and feathered banker if you have a bigger down payment and as the mortgage decreases. But even without a mortgage, your house may still have to appreciate by 6% a year just to break even with taxes, maintenance, and inflation.

Do houses ever appreciate by 6%, 10%, or more? Some places and sometimes, hell yes. But not usually. Typically, house prices keep up with the inflation rate. Granted there are exceptions, since more desirable locations tend to cost more. But even the "hot places" sometimes go down in value. And when this happens, it can destroy many a wet dream.

Consider renting until the market cools. There are many benefits in renting (like low risk, ease in relocating) until you can get a good price on a house and have a large down payment.

And hopefully within ten years of actually buying a house, you'll enjoy paying it off and kicking the mortgage in the nards! Without a mortgage, you have the best chance of your house truly being an investment and a refuge.

<nobolz4IOU$$>

Chapter 32

Write Off The Write Off!

Okay, this is by far one of my favorite slaps upside the head because most people just don't want to understand it for some reason--probably because they're justifying their own ill-advised thinking.

A lot of people brag about their "great tax write-off." I snicker. Don't get me wrong, if you are buying something because you need it and get a tax deduction on the side, that's great. But when your decision to buy something is swayed because you'll get the tax advantage, well that's laughable…and sad. Why? You're spending a dollar to save a quarter.

Mortgages are the biggest scam and robber of your wealth there is. And we're suckered into them because of the tax write off. Sometimes the decision to borrow money to buy a house or to buy a bigger house than is necessary or to not pay off a mortgage early, is based on the old excuse that the mortgage interest is tax deductible.

The math is simple—you give the bank a dollar in interest and in return the government doesn't make you pay tax on it (saving you around twenty-five cents or so). So you just spent a dollar to save a quarter! Get it? This isn't smart or savvy or anything but dumb. You are celebrating saving twenty-five cents, but you've really lost seventy-five cents! This is the oldest trick in the book. Are you really that gullible? Despite this, most people hold on to their mortgage like it is part of the family. Quit falling for it.

A $200,000 mortgage at a 4% annual interest rate sounds modest enough, yet you're still throwing away $6,000 to the bank after the $2,000 tax write off every year. The only good news is that the amount thrown away slowly goes down as you pay down the loan…in 30 years. Can you really afford to throw away so much money? Then why do you do it, a-hole? Because you just have to own a house for the investment, huh? Did you not read the section I wrote about houses not being great investments?

Here's the other important piece that people just don't even think about. When you do your taxes each year, you have a choice to either take the standard deduction or itemize your deductions (itemizing is basically just adding up mortgage interest, property tax, giving to charities, etc.). The standard deduction is usually a pretty respectable amount of money (in 2012 it was almost $12,000 for married couples filing jointly!).

This is the dirt: You can take the standard deduction even if you have no mortgage or any other deductions. But if you itemize you'll have to exceed the amount of the standard deduction before it does you any good. Get it, numb chuck? Unless your mortgage interest and other deductions exceed the standard deduction, you get no bonus tax write off from your stupid mortgage. You've been duped and the bank wins at your expense.

Is it wrong to have a mortgage and take the tax write-off? Nope. If you need a house, or even just want it, fine. But don't use the tax write off as a reason to take the plunge into home ownership, or to keep the mortgage until you need dentures.

If you simply don't want to take this advice and "have to" get a tax deduction, here's the best one…give to charity! You'll get the same tax deduction. You'll still spend a dollar to save a quarter. But this time the dollar goes for something of a worthy cause, not to increase the bank's profit. And you get paid back a quarter in tax savings for being so nice. Now there's a good incentive.

<nobolz4IOU$$>

Chapter 33

Gored By A Rampaging Mortgage

While it's possible to save up to buy a house outright, and I think everyone should do it, most people don't have the balls to hack it out. So aside from doing the 100% down payment plan, here is a guideline for staying out of trouble if you simply must get a mortgage and transfer a lot of your wealth to a greedy bank for most of your life.

MAKES GOOD CENTS:
- Ten-year loan (or shorter).
- Fixed-interest rate loan only and no penalty for early payoff.
- Making extra payments along the way.
- Buying only as big a house as you need.
- Minimum 20% down payment, preferably more.
- Waiting for the right price or moving to a different area.

DUMB ASS:
- Getting a loan for 15 years or longer.
- Adjustable rate loans.
- Balloon payment loans.
- Interest only loans.
- Using a Home Equity Line of Credit (HELOC).
- Making only the minimum payments.
- Buying a house that is so large that some rooms are rarely used.
- Putting down less than 20%.

- Getting "house fever" and overpaying.

Why the big deal about a ten year maximum mortgage? It's doable to buy a home with a ten year home loan. Consider that your grandparents and great-grandparents saved up and paid cash, or they had mortgages that lasted less than ten years (or as little as six). And they raised twice as many kids in a house half the size of what we demand today.

Why do we insist on having a separate bedroom for every child, plus a guest room, office, exercise room, and a pet room for Fido? It's asinine. Usually the mortgage grows larger as the house grows larger. So buy a house that meets your needs and budget. Otherwise you'll be paying for the monster-sized residence for the rest of your life. Don't forget that the mortgage interest, taxes, insurance, maintenance, and utilities go up with the size of the house too. And it's harder to re-sell.

These days people put as little as possible down, forcing an additional cost called mortgage insurance. The bank requires this "extra" loan expense unless the buyer brings at least a 20% down payment to the table. Mortgage insurance protects the bank from losing money—not you. You get nothing from it. So don't pay for their peace of mind. Instead bring a jaw-dropping sized down payment to the closing (for somewhere around 20% to 100%). Do you have the shit to wait until then?

When you are ready to buy, take your time and do not overpay. Try not to romanticize about how great life would be to live in that house...or you may agree to shell out too much rather than lose the dream. House fever has moved in. It's harder to pay off a mortgage in ten years when you overpaid at the beginning. Wait for the right house at the right price, no matter how long it takes. Or consider moving to an area where houses cost less.

Tape this on your Neanderthal forehead: If you cannot pay off the house in ten years, then it's a case of too much house, too little money put down, or too much money paid for it! Don't do it.

Oh, and one more very important thing. Your home is NOT an emergency fund. Don't let some bank officer ever talk you into doing a Home Equity Line of Credit (HELOC). Why risk your home for anything? The small savings on interest does not out weigh the risk of losing your "four wall" investment. Don't do a HELOC. Otherwise you just volunteered to take decades to pay off the car, vacation, cell phone, and lattes.

<nobolz4IOU$$>

Chapter 34

Four Wall Venture

Your investment and work evacuation plan (retirement) accounts should be worth more than your house. Yet chances are that your house is your largest asset. And you're the largest ass if you're making this mistake.

Don't let tough times or retirement force the sale of your home. Selling it is fine if you want to do it, but not if you are forced into it. If you confuse your house with a retirement account, someday you may have to sell your home to simply pay the bills.

Bigger houses are also more difficult to sell when the housing market is down and may lose more value than a modest-sized house.

On the flip side, buying too small a house may also force you to sell it when your family quickly outgrows it. You'll have to buy something bigger and throw more money at closing costs, realtor fees, and other unknowns. Use your head for something besides a hat rack.

Forget the whole fucking "starter home" or "house ladder" scam. Those lines were invented by realtors, not by smart investors. It's just a gimmick to get you to buy too dumpy or too small, so you'll buy too often as you work your way up into bigger and bigger homes. Many realtors only care about their own sorry ass and their commissions (which is a huge reason to give you advice that's more to their benefit than yours). What you should do is just keep saving to buy the right house.

It is much smarter to buy a reasonably sized house (not too big, not too small) that will meet your needs for the long haul and stay there, maybe for a lifetime. Remember the modest size house that your grandparents probably raised more kids in? Why isn't that good enough for Your Highness? Anticipate your growing family and buy the size of house that would be the best fit. If you move and buy another house somewhere, always stay with a modest-sized house. That way there's always money left over to save for retirement, too.

If you can't afford what you need now, then don't settle for the wrong house. Wait. Keep renting. Or consider living in a different area. While the realtor will appreciate the commission on you buying and then selling the mistake, along with buying the right house later on too, your retirement fund could probably use the money more than your realtor.

Compared to fifty years ago, house sizes are growing, family sizes are shrinking, divorce rates are increasing, and the average person has less wealth. Hello dipshits! Maybe our families would be closer if we lived closer together and were forced to talk and share meals together. Maybe we'd have more money too. Just a thought...

<nobolz4IOU$$>

Chapter 35

The Renting Scam Sham

Let's beat this dead horse a little more. Home ownership does not automatically guarantee that you will build wealth or become financially secure. Don't even fall for this myth. You might do better by renting for a while, even permanently.

Are you gasping and sputtering that this is stupid advice, because renters throw a lot of money away in rent? Frequently, people who have a large mortgage throw away more money in interest alone than renters pay for the entire rent bill.

Listen up bunghole. Why would you feel better about the bank taking all your money while you take all the risk of home ownership, than a landlord taking some of your money with no risk?

If you jump into buying a house with borrowed money, for many years most of your payment will go to the bank as interest. Much of the remainder of your payment will go towards property taxes and insurance. And that doesn't even include the maintenance or upgrade costs that you'll be forking out. It will be many years before you are building "equity." Don't be fooled like you are by all those infomercials.

Homes are damn expensive ventures. Buy a house for other reasons (like for "nesting", putting down roots, raising your family) and even then, don't overbuy. And don't buy a house if you plan to move within the next five years.

Rent until you have a huge down payment, a big emergency fund, can afford the expenses that come with home ownership, and can still save big towards your job evacuation plan (retirement). Until that time arrives, there's no shame in renting.

Yes, you will "throw" some money away renting, but it's by far less than what you'll be throwing away with a mortgage, taxes and insurance, and an outright loss if the housing market tanks and you are forced to sell and move for work. It's a lot easier, cheaper, and quicker to break out of a lease or rental agreement, than it is to sell a house.

So don't be a naive jerkoff who is in a hurry to jump from a rental into a house. Always remember that you are a savvy investor and factor in RISK. Sometimes the smart choice is to keep renting and sock away the extra money.

<nobolz4IOU$$>

Chapter 36

Using Red To Stay In The Black

Several years ago my wife was driving home in her car "Red" when they were rear-ended. Although she ended up getting whiplash, my wife cried more about the damage to Red. While the drive train and engine were fine, our insurance company totaled the nine-year old car due to what I considered to be relatively minor body damage.

Red was reliable, got forty miles per gallon, and was a one-owner car. Plus my wife loved that car. Still, Red was not worth on paper what she was worth to us. It would be difficult to find another car that good for the insurance value on Red.

It was not a good time to lose Red. First, she was paid for and in excellent condition. Second, we didn't have the money to go buy another car. Third, we did not want a car payment.

But here's the kicker. The car was valued at about $4,900. We had a mechanic friend rough out the rear corner and replace the tail light assembly for about $400. After we bought the car back from the insurance company for $500 and paid our mechanic, we had a perfectly functional car and $4,000 in our pocket.

Yes, the car had a big ugly wart. It always bugged me. Ever since Red was totaled, I continually offered to have the roughed out corner fixed so Red looked like new again. We had to decide: Our pride or money in the bank. My wife didn't see the point of fixing the car body, since Red wouldn't drive any differently or add to our net worth if fixed.

Five years later we were still driving totaled Red without doing anything more than regular maintenance on her. Initially, keeping Red was part of our "get out of debt" plan. After reaching that goal, it was part of our "pay off the house" plan. Then after mailing the final mortgage payment, it was part of our "we have other things we'd rather spend money on" plan.

Not long ago we finally sold Red because my wife found a classic Mustang GT on Craigslist. We paid cash on the spot after test driving it. Very sweet car! She's a keeper. My wife too.

So would you drive a "Red" to save money during a financial storm? How about an older, paid-for car? You can save a fortune by putting down your pride and driving slightly older rigs. No shit.

<nobolz4IOU$$>

Chapter 37

Gouging Gadgets

Would you trade having all of the latest gadgets that you can buy throughout your lifetime to be the oldest person still working at the office? Huh, old geezer? Technology is great, but no amount of stereos or cell phones is worth an extra five-year sentence at the office.

Remember how dazzling and expensive compact disc and video disc players were when they first came out? Or the flip style cell phones? Thanks to hi-tech advances, this technology is now old school and dirt cheap.

Many of us turn up our noses at equipment that is a few years too old technology. This is exactly when you should be buying it. Don't be a pansy about this.

You'll save a bundle, year after year, if you buy slightly older technology in phones, computers, tablets, televisions, video players, game players, and such. Don't run to the store when some new gadget gets released. Always stay a few years behind the latest "thing." You can always find brand new, slightly older technology in the stores or even used (like on Craigslist).

This approach is not peanuts – unless you mean a house-sized pile of them. Do the math. What you save could pay for some amazing vacations or allow you to retire earlier. Every dollar you don't spend now could be ten that you don't have to work for later. Wrap your barbarian mind around that for a change.

Next time you browse in the electronics store, think "I may be working until I'm seventy if I buy this bauble like some boneheaded baboon."

<nobolz4IOU$$>

Chapter 38

Bargain Brain Blitz

Have you ever "impulsed" and bought a bunch of things that you really didn't need or even like that much, simply because they're on sale? Think this isn't a big deal? Better start paying attention, because your wallet is getting cleaned out and I'm sure your garage is already stuffed full.

Most things end up on the bargain rack because they aren't selling. Get it? If the store wants rid of something so badly, why are you in such a hurry to take it home? Chances are this "treasure" is near the expiration date, badly made, beyond ugly, or a clever looking (but useless) invention! If you wouldn't pay full price for the widget, then put it down and walk away, dork brain.

The shopaholic in you gets "happy" endorphins from these buying binges. It's an addiction. Regrettably the buzz only lasts for a few blissful hours after conquering the store…it's gone long before the bill arrives in the mail. So you go out hunting for another "fix." That's exactly how things begin to clutter your home and take up space. There are cheaper and healthier approaches to getting endorphins, like running across a freeway wearing a blindfold!

What happens when these "great deals" and "happy moments" come home and sit on a shelf? Eventually they end up in the garage. When you're sick of parking on the street, they'll end up in the next garage sale, given or thrown away.

Before you buy anything, bargain or not, determine whether it is a want or a need. Think whether you have something similar already at home. Stop buying stuff just because it's cheap. And if you're not sure whether it's an impulse, then it is. Walk away. If you found it followed you home, then make it go back to where it belongs. Pretend your kid stole it and go marching back to the store with it.

There's one last thing to consider here. Anticipation truly can be the best part of the buying process. Most people get bored with a new gadget just after a couple days, and then they start looking for a new adrenaline rush. Instead of continually rushing to the finish line, learn to enjoy the journey.

It's about being satisfied with what you have, and savoring each new thing. If you don't enjoy it several months after purchasing it, maybe it was a mistake to buy it. Return the "error" if possible, and don't make the same blunder again! Got it, bargain breath?

<nobolz4IOU$$>

Chapter 39

Cheap Shots

Buy things used or cheap if they're going to get quickly worn out, rapidly outgrown, easily broken, devoured by hungry teenagers, rarely used, or you don't intend to keep them long. Sometimes it's just fine to be a cheap assed cheapskate. Here are some examples of stuff to go cheap on.

Baby and kids clothes – Kids outgrow their clothes fast. So there's lots of like-new and quality made children's clothing being sold at garage sales and through internet listings. The prices are amazingly low! Your kids won't know any better for years.

Kid's toys – Most toys from your childhood long ago ended up in the dump. And the same thing will probably happen with the toys that your kids play with. Depressing, huh? Although cleverly packaged to impress you, most toys will hardly be played with before being given or thrown away. It's a lot less painful to break a gizmo that was bought used, rather than full price. Your kids won't always know the difference.

Bikes for adults – If you probably won't use a bike often, then go cheap and get it at a garage sale. Why do you think there are so many bikes at garage sales anyway? Many people think they're going to get in shape together, only to be sidelined on the couch with a bag of chips and another crappy sitcom. My wife and I scored some great bikes at garage sales and used them for years before finally splurging on some quality, new ones because we actually discovered we do ride them.

Ski equipment – This hobby can be so expensive. Yet there are dirt cheap prices for just slightly older clothing and gear to be found at ski swaps. And still in perfectly good condition. Unless you plan on Olympic downhill racing, don't waste your money on new ski equipment.

If you'll use your brain for this task half as much as you do for blowing all your money faster than a sailor on shore leave, the possibilities are endless. For anything and everything else you may need, there are garage sales and Craigslist. And, of course, only pay cash!

<nobolz4IOU$

Chapter 40

Quality Rip Offs

Splurge on high quality if you are buying something that you intend to keep, use a lot, and enjoy for a long time. There are times when the least costly approach in the beginning actually costs more in the end. Sometimes being a tightwad actually costs you a big wad.

If you buy a lower-quality version to save a dollar, then it's likely that you won't enjoy the item as much. If settling isn't good for your home's foundation or for your man boobs, how could it be good for your pocketbook? In the long run it costs more to keep buying flimsily-made items that break, rather than buying a single one that will last and truly satisfy.

Over the years I have purchased a string of bottom-of-the-line guitars that I never should have purchased because of their less than enviable sound. After the buyer's fever faded and the rose-tinted glasses fell off, each guitar was eventually sold and replaced with another "bargain" hopeful. It took me three low-priced (but ultimately more expensive) acoustic guitars to learn my lesson. What a dick! What a waste.

Eventually, I saved long enough to purchase an amazing acoustic guitar. The sad thing is, I could have easily brought home a quality guitar years ago if I'd waited a little while longer to save up for the guitar that had both the sound quality and workmanship to last a lifetime.

And so it is with many other items like tools, furniture, appliances, clothes, and even vehicles.

Women too. Hold out for a quality version if you want to keep it forever. Then get the best deal you can.

<nobolz4IOU$$>

Chapter 41

Make The Dog Think He's Next

Think of the neighbor who has twelve junk cars sitting in their backyard, none of which is running….and there still wouldn't be a working model if all of the parts were put together. They are convinced that junkyard is gold. Are you chuckling because you know exactly who that neighbor is? Surprise! Some people think it's you. And maybe your junkyard is located inside of your house.

How many coins, antiques, electronics, trading cards, bobble heads, knick-knacks, dolls, pictures, kitchen gadgets, tools, recreational vehicles, and such does a person need? Frankly you don't need any of it. It's just icing on the cake. And a gut-wrenching diarrhea storm is in store unless you learn to put down the fork before the whole cake is gone too. Have you told yourself to put down the fork and close your big pie hole when it comes to such things?

People often think their stuff will someday be a treasure, or that somehow they're amassing this big fortune in collectables. Get a clue, numb nuts! Whether sold during good times or tough times, most of these so called "investments" are only worth a fraction of the original cost. Even during good times, this stuff isn't making you rich. But in tougher times, they won't be in demand—you'd be lucky to sell for a fraction of what you paid, if at all.

There is a point when "more" stuff is no longer fun, fulfilling or enjoyable. This habit can be harmful to your financial future. So limit the size of your junkyard.

You may need to hold an impressive yard sale that makes the dog scared that he's the next to go.

If you currently have that "golden junkyard," whether it is cars, collectables, gadgets, or other things, here's what to do about it:

Sell off portions of your junkyard – it's just money that's been tied up. Get the freaking money out of it while you can.

Sell anything that you don't use or need.

Sell anything you have payments on, unless it will be paid off in a few months.

Apply all this money to debt and/or put it in your savings and investments.

And if someday ever rolls around and you need that widget that you got rid of, you can always borrow it, rent it, or buy it again--likely for less than what you sold the old one for.

<nobolz4IOU$$>

Chapter 42

Boosted

Many people won't let go of stuff because someday they may need it. So it fills the garage, basement, shed, and overflows to a rented storage unit. Even with triple garages and massive houses, we still need storage units. Too much money is tied up in things we don't use--and we often pay more to store our junk than what it is worth. Does this seem rational? Has your common sense been lost under the heap of shit in the storage unit?

Our home is small by today's standards, yet my wife and I refuse to rent a storage unit. If something doesn't fit inside our house or garage, then it's gone! And both cars must be able to fit inside the garage. That limits the "overflow" into the garage.

If something hasn't been picked up in a year, then it probably won't ever see the light of day until it's liberated. Either we sell it cheap or give it away. While it hurts at first, letting go of things has become easy with practice.

This "letting go" policy even applies to clothing. Quite often the impulse to buy goes away when pondering what's hanging in the closet that must go away to make space for the incoming ones. This policy even has our daughter concerned that someday she may have to give up her bed. Since she uses it every day, this is not likely. Still….if she turns to sleeping on the sofa, this is a possibility!

Try adopting this simple rule for stuff – if you rarely use it or don't have room, then blow it out your ass! Bet you'll like the results so much that this rule is the one thing that you never let go of.

<nobolz4IOU$$>

Chapter 43

All That Turns To Rust

Nearly everything that you buy goes down in value as soon as it's brought home. Most "collectibles" are only collectible when it comes to attracting dust. Try reselling that thing and you'll find out it's no longer "in style," worth less than what you paid…or simply worthless.

So if you want to sell some of this stuff, then what? Often people price their used item like it's new and then wonder "what the fuck?" when they can't unload it. Now their "treasure" is actually a millstone around their neck. Potential buyers don't care what it's worth to you or what you paid for it. They want a deal. The question is whether you have the balls to take what you can get for it—and not what you think it's worth.

Here are some tips for selling stuff quick. Usually that sweet spot for pricing is one quarter to one half the price of new. If it's in excellent shape and fairly new, you may get half of what you paid. But be flexible on the price. Do you want some cash in your hand or not?

Around half price is where people tend to "cross-over" and consider buying new to get every original part, instructions, warranty, and the ability to return it if it's defective. So the asking price of a used item must be sweet enough for someone to be willing to give up some things and take some risks.

If an item looks "slightly or somewhat used," then ask for one quarter to one third of what you paid. If you've had your fun with it, slash the price just to get rid of it. Don't you love it when you get a great deal on

something? Let someone else have their day in the sun.
That can be fun, too. Or better yet, give it away. After
all, what comes around goes around.

<nobolz4IOU$$>

Chapter 44

Home Holiday

Have you ever come back from vacation feeling frustrated because it takes so much effort to pack and unpack several times, travel for hours or days, have less than classy accommodations, and then eat a lot of bad food? Stay vacations are relaxing because they avoid these pitfalls.

The best thing about vacations is escaping from work. So why spend hours driving somewhere in order to "start" vacationing? Relax at home and begin the vacation from the moment that you leave work. During your vacation you can even drive by the office a few times, gaze at the losers stuck there, and flip the bird out the window (disguise recommended for this).

Consider that hotels usually have dubious cleaning, pathetic televisions, lumpy beds, cramped living areas, no sound system, and a token microwave to "cook" with. Why pay a premium to stay in such a natty place when you have a comfy place at home that won't cost a dime extra?

Plus, you have insider knowledge of the best places to see, things to do, and top places to eat in your local area and have access to childcare that you trust. Freedom from the wee-ones for a date is a rare vacation treat.

So ponder how refreshing it would feel to do the following:

- Turn off the phone and sleep until noon.
- When you finally get out of bed, do nothing responsible or worthwhile.
- Hire someone to clean your place and the only finger you lift is to write out the check.
- Hand the kids over to the sitter, then go to the movies.
- Hit some local sporting events.
- Treat yourself to a pedicure, manicure, facial, and massage.
- Leave a pitcher filled with ice water and limes sitting on the counter to enjoy as you walk aimlessly through the house.
- Read worthless books, gab on the phone, and treat a friend to lunch.
- Eat at the three-star restaurant that your friends are raving about.

If you skip the hotel and travel expenses, you can afford massive pampering and still have vacation money left over. Plus you are seen by friends (and enemies) while enjoying the first-class treatment. Nice, huh?

Playing hooky at home feels very relaxing and quite naughty. Try it and you'll see!

<nobolz4IOU$$>

Chapter 45

Vacationing With The Natives

There are other times when relaxing at home sounds blah. It's time for an adventure! So throw a dart at a map or your spouse's globe of an ass, pick a spot, and go.

The best bet is running away to a place within driving distance. Surely there are lots of appealing places near you to get away to. It's quick and economical too. Plus, nothing busts a getaway faster than a canceled flight that leaves you far from home and adventure.

When you find a spot and a hotel that you love, keep going back to it. Mention that it's a special getaway when making the reservation or checking in, and you may get upgraded for no extra charge. And ask to be added to the hotel's e-mail list, so you find out about special deals.

Sometimes it is cheaper and easier to use a travel website. Try all of the approaches, but still call the hotel direct before booking online. Often they can beat an internet deal or they will throw in freebies. And don't you love getting stuff de gratis?

While it saves a lot by traveling off season, the biggest perk is simply the absence of the crowds. Still, if you enjoy being crowded, by all means go during the high season and pay more to get less service!

Locals know the best things to do and see in the area, so put down your macho pride and I-don't-need-directions arrogance and ask around. Don't rely on tourist brochures to find your way around. A glittery ad does not equal fab food or fun diversions. Don't believe everything that's in print (unless it's in this book).

Locals also know where to eat, so ask which eateries are the hidden gems. Remember this is an adventure trip, so be an explorer. Sometimes driving around town is the best lead to where the good grub is to be found. If there's a bunch of cars parked outside of a tacky looking restaurant, then there is mouth watering food to be found inside. Ugly buildings do not attract hungry people the way that greasy, fatty food makes ugly people, but I digress.

Avoid chain restaurants unless you enjoy paying a premium for food that is somewhere between mediocre slop and pathetic upchuck. Eat breakfast on the cheap. Wolf down cold cereal and fruit in the room, graze like a cow at the hotel's free buffet, or drive like you stole it to the local grocery store or bakery.

Lunch is the best deal when eating out. Order a large lunch and stash the leftovers in the refrigerator in your room. Dinner is now a cinch. If leftovers aren't your thing, then split a plate for dinner with your partner. Do this more often than not, or your pants will probably be snugger around the waist (yet looser around the back wallet pocket) upon your return home. And that's the shits!

As a side note, ask friends and family that live in interesting locations if they would be interested in doing a home exchange. Swapping places with strangers can be scary (especially if you're talking about spouse swapping). Swapping with people you know and trust eliminates the concern about who will be in your home.

Now run away from home for a while…

<nobolz4IOU$$>

Chapter 46

Prepaid Nightmares

While it sounds cool to "pre-pay" for your vacations, do not buy a timeshare unless you want to overpay for vacations the rest of your life, like a bimbo with a credit card at the makeup counter.

Timeshares are designed to take money from your wallet and plunk it into the timeshare's bank account. Simple wealth transfer. Salespeople talk so excitedly about timeshares in hopes of landing a big commission check (which will be paid for with your money).

Buying a timeshare is not the end of your lodging expenses, either. It is just the beginning. Timeshare "owners" pay maintenance and cleaning fees forever. These costs alone would pay for a week-long vacation at a nice hotel every year. When was the last time you stayed at a hotel and found an itemized expense on the receipt for maintenance or cleaning fees? Never, right? Keep it that way, dog breath.

And investments are supposed to go up in value, right? Think through selling your timeshare down the line…ask the salesperson why it's a good idea to buy a timeshare when you would be lucky to get half the purchase price in the resale market. Wait for their answer…wait for it…

If you have not stormed out of their closing office yet, do so now with dramatic ferocity. Rip up the paperwork in front of them for an even more spectacular flair and demand your fifty-dollar gift card.

Even if you ignore the salespeople's horrific math and find yourself sitting through the entire presentation, don't sign on the dotted line. And don't buy a discounted timeshare (from a desperate owner) on the resale market either. The maintenance fees are still an endless bad deal. Plus, think about the hassle of having to arm wrestle with the other "owners" for a room when you want it.

If you like to wing your vacations (because you never plan anything and obviously not your finances either or you wouldn't own a timeshare in the first place), then finding an available room in a timeshare will be a huge problem. Usually timeshares only set up one resort in a town. So if that resort is booked up when you want to stay there, then you'll be renting some type of other lodging anyway.

Why limit yourself to the limited timeshare options when there are hotels, motels, and everything in between all over the place? That's just plain nuts.

So now that you have promised never to buy a timeshare, don't get sucked into a "fractional ownership" arrangement either. They are similar to timeshares, the difference being that it's a small group of strangers that buy a property together. Do you really want to bet your money that the other owners can pay their loans and maintenance fees? Avoid "fractionals" like your Aunt Sue's prune jubilee fruit cake—there's just too much that can go wrong.

And if anyone in your family suggests buying a vacation house together, politely decline (re-read the previous Bitch Slap on that subject). This would likely turn into a headache of Grand Canyon proportion. Eventually someone will want to sell their portion, and the other party won't be able to buy them out. Imagine how nice the next Thanksgiving meal will taste after that conversation…

There is a smart way to pre-pay your vacation. Plunk some money into an investment (like Treasury Bonds) that is known for safety, yet gives a modest yet steady yield. Then use the growth to pay for future vacations forever and stay wherever you like. Did you catch the part where you keep the money at the end of the day? Bet that will break your heart!

<nobolz4IOU$$>

Chapter 47

Paper Weight

To some people, acquiring stuff is the goal in life. Quite often our goal of climbing the property ladder takes us up the company ladder towards a big pay increase. All in hopes of buying the biggest house we can afford and dragging home lots of impressive stuff to fill it so we can impress loser friends. Nothing says little pee wee like a big Hummer in the driveway.

While I'm not against having stuff or spending some afternoons polishing a smoking hot sports car, I detest being a slave to my stuff or my job.

The more stuff you have, the less time you will have to enjoy it. It takes extra time on the job to pay for things. And it takes your spare time to clean, wash, vacuum, wax, paint, repair, maintain, and upgrade the gadgets. Yep, all your stuff will require most all your time on and off the job.

My wife and I told our four year old daughter that we didn't have to do anything we didn't want to do. She quickly replied "That's not true, you have to work." She was right and the truth hurt. But we don't work nearly as much as our neighbors do.

Don't buy something if you'll have to work lots of overtime or take an extra job just to make the minimum payments. Don't buy it if making the payment will be tighter than those pants that shrunk in the dryer and make you sing like a soprano. Don't buy it if you'll spend more time taking care of it than actually enjoying it.

Please get this! Don't have everything you own dependent on keeping your income at its current (or getting it to a higher) level. This kind of burden adds a lot of pressure and stress. It makes you stuck at your job. And for what? More stuff that you have little time to enjoy as you climb the "success" ladders? It's not worth it.

What if you can't accept a dream job or move to some really cool place because it requires a small pay cut? This will make you dislike and resent everything that held you back.

If you want to have more spare time and money, and be less pressured by your job, then stop buying so much crap. Stop and take a big ass laxative. Dump everything that doesn't add notably to your life. Don't let the spoils from your past spoil your future.

<nobolz4IOU$$>

Chapter 48

Wander Squander

Many people with money problems predict that they "just need to make more money" and their problems will be solved. If that was true, then your money issues would have disappeared after your last raise. Your denial is the only thing that's not vanishing around here. Your logic has long gone missing.

Here's the big steaming pile you need to pay attention to, lest you step in it with bare feet. Until you learn how to do more with what you have now, more money will simply bring more money problems on a grander scale later. Scoring a raise at work will continue to be "reason" to celebrate by getting one more splurge on something with a sixty month payment plan at 20% interest. The behavior that got you into trouble at one income level, will keep you in trouble at a higher income level. Consider how many lottery and inheritance winners end up broke after a few years.

So when it comes to getting wealthier or simply getting out of debt, it's not how much you make that really matters. It's how much you keep, and how long you've kept it, that matters.

And you have more control over this than you want to admit. Stop blaming your parents, family, boss, education, and such. The only constant thing in the formula is big ol' snot nosed you.

It's time to stop the money hemorrhage and reconsider the "little stuff" that eats away at your wallet. Your problem is not the shark, it's the piranhas.

It's time to tell your money where to go and then make sure it behaves. Making more money or finding another job is probably not the answer. Yes, a bigger shovel helps, but only if you've mastered the little shovel first. Otherwise a bigger shovel only helps you blow a bigger wad faster.

<nobolz4IOU$$>

Chapter 49

Blowing The Bonus

Here's a common mistake—we get a raise at work and celebrate by "upping" our lifestyles and toys. Or we get a gift in cash or a bonus at work, and we go spend it like there's no tomorrow. Just like a drinking binge, we wake up the next day with a hangover, take a strong pain reliever, have an extra hot taco and a beer, and wonder what the fuck we were thinking the night before.

Here's a shocking piece of advice. If you really love blowing things that much, why don't you open a blomenaide stand? Instead of blowing the bonus, blow some boners. At least you'll be getting paid for your services instead of getting banged in the rear at the mall.

Got your attention? Always put the extra money from a raise or cash windfall into your job evacuation plan (retirement), investments, savings, college fund, or debt pay-down. You're used to living on less (supposedly), so keep on doing it. If you can't stomach that, then at least put half of it away for your future. Don't blow it all, or you've blown the chance to get ahead, along with the money.

<nobolz4IOU$$>

Chapter 50

Mirror, Mirror

Now here's a paradox. The rich sometimes look poor and the poor sometimes look rich.

The best book I've read on the lifestyles of the rich (and the pretenders) is called <u>The Millionaire Next Door</u> by Thomas J. Stanley and William D. Danko. This book is a real eye opener. They interviewed millionaires and found a surprising number of them live in modest neighborhoods and drive boring cars. They held onto a surprising amount of their income by evaluating every expense.

Real millionaires ask themselves honest questions. Is this is a need or merely a want?' Will it add value or happiness to my life? How much will it be worth in a few years? And will buying this rob too much from my job evacuation plan (retirement)?

So who then is living in the big house in an exclusive neighborhood, and "paying" for fancy vehicles, expensive toys and vacations? It's likely the lavish wannabe that has big income, but little net worth. Everything they have goes towards the minimum payments on their expensive lifestyle. It's all about impressions. A rich façade, covering a rusty mobile home.

Their impressive house is making them house poor. They are working more hours than they would like to keep up the golden window dressing. Most onlookers envy their dazzling lifestyle and wrongly assume the lavish wannabe's are rich. Nope. And they likely never will be.

Trying to look rich before becoming rich is the surest way to the shithouse. Alternatively, many millionaires got rich by living under their income and saving the difference. And they kept doing this after it literally paid off.

Most people must choose between being rich or proud….at least until they become rich. Then they often no longer give a crap what people think, and decide if something was good enough before, then it's good enough now.

The millionaire down the street is like a "sleeper" car that looks unimpressive, but can outrun anything in the neighborhood. It's time to quit trying to look and act rich when your sorry ass ain't, and focus on becoming rich!

<nobolz4IOU$$>

Chapter 51

Nifty Nerds

We do not know everything. And, sorry to break the bad news Mr. Knowitall, you do not know everything either. Even if you study the rest of your life, you'll never learn everything there is to know. And that's okay, because someone you already know is probably a nerd about things that you are clueless about.

The real juice is acknowledging the limits of what you know. If you have a stick shoved so far up your ass that you refuse to ask for advice, you'll look (and buy) like a clueless, spineless schmuck at the store. Ask for help, and only your pride takes a hit. Either way your pride is getting smashed up, so limit the other damage to your wallet!

Do not be afraid to ask for tips at unlikely places and times, because there are hidden nerds within most people. Remember those scrawny geeks in gym class that you and your buddies gave wedgees and swirlies to? Well, they used their talents for something more than slapping the monkey and choking the dolphin. Now they're all grown up and out there working like you. Except they're smarter.

Such are the nerds and geeks of all types: Computer nerds, car freaks, cell phone maniacs, electronics mutants, music nuts, right at your fingertips! Bet that guy behind the electronics counter at the big box store probably knows a thing or two about the latest gadgets. I bet a lot of your co-workers have a lot of exotic and hi-tech hobbies.

We have some co-workers that are freaking brilliant computer nerds, and they don't even work in the high-tech field. They just live and breathe this stuff for fun after work hours. Before we buy computer stuff or electronics, we do a huddle with at least one of them and get their opinion. Bet you know someone like that, or someone else that seems to have amazing luck with finding good deals on cool gadgets and gizmos.

People are interesting, especially when their opinion is outside of your area of interest. The more friendly advice obtained the better! So ask around and make informed decisions before you buy a big splurge item.

Let a nerd make you look good. Just hope he wasn't in your gym class, or you may find yourself the proud new purchaser of a big screen television, high end music system, half a dozen cell phones, and two top notch computers when he lifts your credit card number and uses his nerd talents to charges it all to you and get away with it cleaner than a quick swirly.

<nobolz4IOU$$>

Chapter 52

Time Warped

Time for a little nostalgia. It's hard to imagine ourselves growing old when we are young. So we fail to plan or save or make time for people in our lives, because we have the "plenty of time to get to that" attitude. And so we blow it off.

Then the time warp hits and tomorrow you celebrate turning forty. After dragging yourself home from work, the kids talk excitedly about friends and things they did that day. Your spouse is moaning about the latest scheme their nemesis pulled at work. After grabbing the remote control and turning on the TV, you tell them "not now." The evening news does a spiel about saving for the kids' college and retirement, but the anchor quickly moves on to another story and the warning fades with it.

You blink and it's your fiftieth birthday. The gag gift from your wife, a bicycle horn on a cane with a banner proclaiming "old geezer crossing" didn't help your mood. Where did the years go? John is home on break from college and for once not asking for the car keys….and you promised to help Emily fill out a student loan application tomorrow. It hasn't been that long since you helped John do the same thing and it was torture. Tomorrow is going to be ugly. Instead of enjoying birthday cake with family and friends, you're hiding out in the office breathing into a paper bag while staring at overdue credit card bills and your meager retirement portfolio.

Another ten years flashes by. In a moment of introspection, your wife asks what you would have done differently. After glancing at the grandkids' photos, you answer "a lot" before dashing out the door for work. Could this be your sucky life?

<nobolz4IOU$$>

Chapter 53

For Sale: Time

Like whores, we trade our time and ultimately our lives for money. That's the harsh and depressing reality. Would you drag yourself to work and put up with everyone's shit if there wasn't some pocket change in it for you? Yet piles of money won't add any more days to your life. If you want more time for yourself, then you're going to have to trade your left nard for it.

Consider working fewer hours at your job, so you have more time to dick off. This will make a direct hit to the checkbook. Most likely you can't work less hours if you're up to your eye sockets in debt. Get out of debt, and then you can stop working forty plus hours a week. Unless you really hate your job, talk to your employer before looking for another job. Many businesses welcome the idea of cutting back to save money while keeping a skilled employee.

A second way to buy more time is to pay someone to do things for you. No, I don't mean a whore--get your mind out of the gutter. Sometimes trading your money for time is a freaking brilliant idea. My wife and I haven't cleaned our house in years, yet it magically gets cleaned every two weeks thanks to our cleaning lady. Now our castle is a place of refuge. While we are capable of slinging a mop and vacuum cleaner around, and have plenty, we don't particularly enjoy it. And I'll be fucked if I'm going to give up my Saturdays cleaning the bloody house. Why not hire out a few of the chores that you really don't like doing?

The third way to "buy" more time is to trade stuff for it. I am not against having things. I'm against stuff that requires working a ridiculous number of hours to pay the bill, especially when the bloody item will also soak up your "free" time to maintain it. I've beat this dead horse already.

The amount of free time that you have is directly related to how much shit you have to take care of. So sell, downsize, trade, and get rid of anything that sucks up your time like a black hole. Less stuff means less work needed to pay for it and less time needed to take care of it. You'll actually be getting more time and saving money. It's like a hard on that doesn't go to waste.

Always be looking for ways to work less, hire out detested chores, and have less stuff that just clutters your world. Voila! Now there's more time to hang with the people that matter the most to you. No, I'm not talking about your grown up asshole siblings.

<nobolz4IOU$$>

Chapter 54

Job Evacuation Plan

Too often the word retirement conjures up images of withdrawn and bored old geezers that are past their usefulness and waiting to die like an old racehorse put out to pasture. Their dicks must not be able to get hard anymore, no matter how much Viagra they pop. Depressing, huh?! Maybe so few people plan for retiring, because it sounds so awful.

Maybe a change in perspective will remove the mental roadblocks that are holding you back. Consider that maybe this is really the case: Exiting the boring work scene is when you will feel the most useful and alive. Finally all of your time will be devoted to doing your pet projects (and not your boss'). You can volunteer your time to help others, visit family, sleep in, take a physics class, or see the world.

And it's totally your call as to when you stop working at the day job. If you love your job, then keep turning in the timecards until it stops being fun. Don't let the government, your employer, or anyone else pick the right time for you to move on to better things. Not everyone wants to wait to retire until Social Security kicks in. If you want to evacuate the work site at age sixty or much earlier, then figure out what it will take and kick it in the ass.

But whatever you do, don't keep waiting to get the ass kicking plan rolling or the timeline will have to roll with it too.

So what's your "job evacuation plan?"

<nobolz4IOU$$>

Chapter 55

A Loser Millionaire

Time mixed with money invested, makes people wealthy without much effort.   No fucking kidding. Why don't they engrain this into our heads at school like they do reading, writing, and arithmetic (why the hell do they call it the three "R's")? The key is to start saving and investing early. Even a meager amount put aside each month will do, and the more the better.

On the flip side, procrastination, followed by greed and impatience are dangerous friends to hang with. Don't plug money into any wild investments, or you will risk losing the profit and the entrance fee into the game. A solid investment goes up in value without exposing the owner's throat to the wolves.

Take a serious look at index funds and mutual funds, rather than individual stocks. You have to spread the risk wider than a whore's pimply legs at an open house.

Most people won't become wealthy without investing in the stock market in some manner, and it's really not that hard to do. Yes there is real estate and starting a small business, but most people don't have the balls or brains for either of those. Merely saving money and investing in the stock market over time will do it for most.

If you saved just $100 per month and invested it into an index fund or mutual fund yielding an 8% average annual return from age 20 to 70 years old, you could have almost $800,000! Keep in mind that the

United States stock market return has historically been greater than 10% average annually since the 1930's.

Increase your savings to $300 dollars per month. If you could get an 8% average annual return from age 20 to 70, you would have about $2.4 million! If you invested $300 per month from age 20 to 70 and got a 10% average annual return on your money, then you would have over $5 million!

All this for fucking peanuts, you dumb shit. All from just saving some cable TV and cell phone and latte money over your lifetime. The piranhas, not the sharks, man! Imagine if the stock market return is stellar some of those years....the work evacuation plan could be executed way earlier than hoped!

<nobolz4IOU$$>

Chapter 56

The Shovel Syndrome

Sometimes people don't give others credit for building up an impressive savings stash, because "they earn so much money." Bullshit. Like that made it easy for them to not spend everything like a drunken sailor. Sorry, but that excuse is ridiculous. Lots of big income earners blow all they make....just like many lottery winners and people who suddenly inherit money do. Income level has nothing to do with the savings level— or the United States Government would have no debt.

On the other greasy hand, people with small shovels don't always get respect for their sparse savings. Consider your single income friends and families who work overtime and sacrifice to scrape together extra money, after paying for housing, utilities, and food. Add some kids into the formula and the math looks Greek. As much as we love them, children are expensive!

Perspective is an amazing thing. Whenever you get cocky, remember that someone else has done more with less. Then your excuses fly right out the proverbial window. More like out your ass. Many lower income folks save a higher percentage of their income than higher income people do. You can learn a lot from that kind of diligence and drive.

It takes some impressive self-denial, guts, and drive to even pick up a shovel. It's less important if your shovel is big or small, than whether you are shoveling greenbacks onto the right pile.

<nobolz4IOU$$>

Chapter 57

Slow Motion At Fast Forward

Is the money that lands in your checking account really yours? If the answer is yes, then how come your savings account is as empty as your skull? Until you decide to keep a piece of every dollar that lands in your wallet, then it will mysteriously fly away right into someone else's hands. You work hard to earn each paycheck, so work equally hard to keep it. Hold on to more of your paycheck by slowing down your spending.

Spending a dollar here and there will break you. Remember, it's the piranhas, not the sharks, that I'd fear. Don't give away your future one buck at a time! Every time you hand over some money, then you are deciding to work longer to earn those dollars back. It's probably not a conscious thought, and that's the problem.

By not thinking it through, the decision is made by the child inside that screams "I want that toy now!" Too bad the grey haired person that has worked forty years (and still can't afford to retire) is too tired to shout a warning. What he is muttering is quite different and unfit for repeating. On second thought, let's do repeat what the old fart is saying: "My fucking boss; this job blows chucks; the damn government steals everything from me; I can't wait to die."

Don't be that old fuck. Evaluate every purchase by asking "Do I want to work longer for this?" Well, do you?

With your spending on slow motion, now you can place 10% or more of each pay check into your savings account and job evacuation plan (retirement). Think that won't add up to much, so why bother? Bother! This is huge.

Picture yourself in twenty years asking the same question while you're drinking frosty beverages by the pool (while others are still sitting in a poorly-lit cubicle pretending to like the boss). Do you see it? You can shave off years of your work evacuation plan by simply putting your spending on slow motion and saving the difference.

So keep reminding yourself to slow down the buying sprees and save more dough by picturing yourself further down the road….living your life with no time clocks, watches, or schedule.

<nobolz4IOU$$>

Chapter 58

Auto Pilot

Christmas and birthdays happen at the same time every year, numb skull. Yet somehow you're stunned and unprepared when they roll around again. Vehicles need regular tune ups and tires wear out after so many miles. These things are a given, yet you don't sock away something every month so you're ready to pick up the slack when they happen. Why the hell not?

Yes, there is the occasional bad luck, but that's a pathetic excuse too-- that's what emergency funds are for. Too bad most of the messes that you deal with are your own doing. Or lack of doing. Oh, I wish there was a way to shock your sorry ass into becoming a saver— because that's the only hope out of this spin cycle.

You can't save a dollar once it's been spent. So put some money where the sun don't shine, where you can't reach it, before you ever see it. Set up savings and retirement accounts to automatically withdraw money from your checking account. If you never see the money, then you won't miss it or be tempted to spend it.

If it helps, set up separate savings accounts and name each one (like the vacation fund, emergency fund, car replacement, house down payment, my sex change, etc.). While you may consider "borrowing" from the savings account, you are less likely to swipe from a stash named "car replacement fund" to buy concert tickets.

Whenever you get a raise or extra money—do something shocking. Save it. You are supposedly used to living on less already, so it won't feel like a sacrifice. Set up an automatic transfer into savings.

Every month slam 5%-20% of your income away for the future (such as in retirement investments). Set up an automatic transfer.

Consider opening a college saving plan (like a 529 plan) for each of your kids. Set up an automatic transfer.

Put your future on auto pilot, so you can forget the worry and focus on the now.

<nobolz4IOU$$>

Chapter 59

Complimentary Peanuts

After your assortment of investments "cooks" for twenty to forty years, it will start earning more money than you get paid for showing up at your day job. That's the beauty of compounding interest over time! Somewhere around that point you can quit working the day job if you wish, and draw off some "pay" each year from your pile of peanuts. I bet you'd give your left nut to have that. Unfortunately, I doubt there are any takers.

So you're going to have to do some planning. Do you have enough to make that happen or even know how much is enough? Put in the effort now, so that your cash can work for you later.

You may need to get help to consider the effects of inflation, stock market changes, increased insurance and medical expenses, and taxes on your stash. There are many resources available (check the library, internet, and your bank) to help you estimate how much you need to retire, how much you need to save each month to get there, and what the best investment options are for your situation.

Just remember, bozo, diverse investments are the safest route. Don't put all your nuts in one place. And think "slow brew," not "champagne blow out." Eventually the savings, interest, dividends, and such will turn into an impressive stash.

It will be tempting to coast once you're part way there, but don't do it. Keep on adding money every month and don't dip into the growth until you have earned the right, like in having given up your left nut.

<nobolz4IOU$$>

Chapter 60

Generation Extra

Do you realize how different your family tree would look if your forehead wasn't like an ape's? What if you saved and invested throughout your lifetime, died as a multi-millionaire, then passed it on to your children? What if your money-wise kids did the same for their kids, who later did the same thing for their kids? The family tree could put Mr. Trump's comb over to shame.

Along the way you could all live and give like never before. Some great things could be accomplished in the world just because you decided to grow some real balls with money. Now that's a legacy worth leaving.

<nobolz4IOU$$>

Chapter 61

Smoking The Tires

The biggest effect you can have on your future wealth is to work as hard to keep your money, as you did to earn it. This effect is bigger than your annual income or how well the stock market is doing. Think about it – every dollar you waste now will have to be earned again (possibly several times over) before you can afford to quit working. That means working more years than you hoped to.

Here is where the rubber meets the road. If you are determined to change your relationship with money, then the next step is to get serious with the details—like getting a "get out of debt" plan, saving strategy, investment and job evacuation planning, insurance, kid's college fund, and the list may go on.

Read more books on personal finance. Ask for advice from those who have done it already (not from broke friends or family). Seek answers and then make adjustments. There's still time to make your life far different, easier, and better. Get off your ass and do it!

<nobolz4IOU$$>

Chapter 62

Bitch Slap Recap

Okay, you numb nuts. Time to rehash all this shit in hopes it will sink into your fat head. I've summarized the main points from each bitch slap in this bitch slap recap. Please read and ponder these things half as much as you would your favorite slutty romance novel or girly magazine and I guarantee you'll be one up on your neighbors and the rest of your family. Someone needs to take the lead out of the shit hole and back to easy street.

Too much debt robs your choice in how to spend your time.

Cautiously feed the plastic piranhas, and use cash to curb your appetite.

Only invest with your own money, don't borrow trouble.

Steer clear of the outlandish fees and terrible interest rates "offered" by many financial institutions.

Pay yourself big by paying off debt and not borrowing.

Are you fanatical enough to jump-start the financial engine?

Being debt free feels as good as a month of Fridays.

Being a dedicated consumer is good for everyone (except you).

With no debt you can earn less, yet have more left over.

Decide to keep a piece of every dollar that lands in your wallet.

Consistency with a simple plan is everything.

Keep financially fit following a prescribed routine and you'll quit paying the lazy tax.

Use a monthly budget to tell your money where to go.

Cut the expenses that you enjoy the least.

Put frugal "style" into your life.

Cut the hassle factor and expense of grocery shopping.

Some of your strongest critics to change will come disguised as close family and friends.

Look for chances to strengthen your body and relationships at the same time.

Invest your time, heart, and soul into your family and friends – just don't add money to the mix.

Money and relationships only go together if two people are married.

A truly rich person chases the dream that sets their heart free.

Don't try to protect your kids from their own lazy taxes.

Give your kids less stuff, so they learn creativity and determination.

Buying a house at the wrong place, time, and way spoils the dream.

Kick the mortgage to the curb, or you'll spend a buck on interest to save a quarter on taxes.

Hold off on buying a house until you have a 20% down payment and a ten-year, fixed-rate mortgage.

Your investment and job evacuation plan (retirement) portfolio should be worth more than your house.

Sometimes the smart choice is renting and saving the extra money.

Once you pay off the car loan, keep the rig and continue making the car payment—this time into your savings so your next car is paid for with cash.

Be willing to drive an old "Red" all the way into the "black."

Don't let a reverse wealth vehicle (camper or motor home) haul your financial problems around the country.

Always stay a few years behind the latest hi-tech "things."

If you're not sure whether you are buying something to get that shopping "high," then you are.

Buy things cheap or used if they won't be used much.

Splurge on quality if you intend to use something a long time.

During tough times people aren't interested in buying your bobble head collection.

Let go of things that you rarely use or won't fit inside your house.

Used stuff usually goes for one quarter to one half the cost of new.

Playing hooky at home feels very relaxing, quite naughty, and is cheap!

When you need a vacation adventure, stay within driving distance and do what the locals do.

Never buy into timeshares, fractionals, "family shares," or any other type of "vacation-share" property or you'll be sharing something alright – a headache.

Protect your income as diligently as you worked to earn it.

Your stuff owns you big time – forcing you to work, work, work.

How much money you keep and how long you've kept it is more important than the size of your paycheck.

Always toss extra money into your savings or investments, so down the road something extraordinarily big will happen.

Work hard, pay your own way, and don't expect anyone to rescue you.

Trying to look rich before becoming rich is a sure way to stay broke.

Before you buy, the more "nerd advice" you gather the better.

Don't sacrifice your family's security for your macho image.

Time reveals when we've given away too much to things that don't matter.

If you want more time for your family and self, then you're going to have to trade something for it.

Figure out a job evacuation plan, so you can someday pursue your dreams with the time and money necessary to make them happen.

Money and time mixed with a respectable interest rate will make you wealthy without much effort.

It's less important if your shovel is big or small, than whether you are steadily shoveling greenbacks onto the right pile.

Every time you spend a dollar, you are deciding to work longer before putting on a gold retirement watch.

Get off the lazy tax train and cruise on autopilot instead – arrange it so that every month 5%-20% of your income gets slammed away for the future.

After letting your portfolio "cook" for 20 to 40 years, your investments will likely earn more in interest and dividends than what you are getting paid for showing up at your day job.

Don't buy presents that you can't afford…gifts with style and heart are much more impressive than the price tag anyway.

Once the financial pressure is off, allow yourself some sweet rewards, and give generously to others.

Your vision can change the family tree for generations.

There's still time to make your life far different, fulfilling, and better.

Okay. How many ways can I say these things? Do you see any light yet? Or is your head still stuck up your ass so far that the only thing you can see is last night's sauerkraut and hot dog casserole festering like a time bomb? Better get out of there, quick!

<nobolz4IOU$$>

That's All Folks!

Two Last Things For Your Consideration

Thing #1: Your Input Matters

Thank you so much for reading my book. If you enjoyed it, would you be so kind as to leave a review at your favorite online book retailer? Your review may help other curious readers to check out my book! And I'd really appreciate your feedback on all my hard work. Thanks again for your time.

Thing #2: Other Books You Might Enjoy

If you enjoyed this book, chances are you'll enjoy some of these other books as well, currently available as ebooks that are downloadable in just about every format at Smashwords.com, Amazon.com, and your other favorite online retailers. You'll also find the links to all seven of these books at boileddownmoneygoo.com.

Breaching The Guardian Dimension, by Cory Richardson.
Topic: Spokane, Washington area in eighty years. Two girls' relationship, crime, revenge.
Description: Coming of age in the 2090's, friends Marcus, Randi, Vamir and Meagan find themselves working at a prestigious government-funded supernatural research facility. Something goes wrong after Marcus' very first "exposure." His friends watch in disbelief as other employees mysteriously die right after their first exposures. It is not clear whether they're

victims of machine malfunctions, the guardians or something else. During the mayhem, Randi and Meagan find the "something more" in their relationship that Randi has been longing for all along. Like their favorite song, it's para, para, paradise. But something connected to the research program dooms the girls' alliance. WARNING: Contains some adult themes (lesbian encounters), but nothing graphic.

Silicon Facades, by Cory Richardson.

Topic: Depraved coming society, our digital future, and twisted justice.

Description: How our online presence in the early 2000's evolved into the government's digital social tool of the 2130's to pigeonhole citizens into social classes and control their every activity, even where babies come from. In 2133, Darren and his pregnant wife, Amber, a smart, drop dead stunning, blue-eyed brunette, desperately seek ingenious and mostly criminal methods to raise their status, having dropped to the lowest social class because of circumstances affecting their government issued Score. Take the roller coaster ride with the exploits of Darren and Amber and their shocking nonconformist ways of playing against the system's outrageous rules.

Money Prick, The Harsh Truth Your Friends Don't Have The Balls Or Brains To Tell You, by Taylor Young.

Topic: Personal finances with a crass humor spin.

Description: You're in luck. You just found the most enjoyable, hilarious book you'll ever read on a typically not-so-fun topic; family/personal finances. Even if you know all this stuff already, it's worth reading just for the laughs! WARNING: If you are offended by some crass language, then maybe this book isn't for you.

How I Lost A Million Dollars Twice, And Other Brilliant Adventures, by Taylor Young.

Topic: Personal finance tales you'll shake your head over.

Description: Through a bizarre twist of circumstances, follow Taylor's eclectic accounts of kissing goodbye a couple million dollars by a ripe ol' young age. Enjoy someone else's misery while you learn what not to do with your time and money thanks to Young's numb skull, painful lessons. Maybe some of these things can save your butt from a good kicking. WARNING: If you are offended by some crass language, then maybe this book isn't for you.

No Good Deed Goes Unpunished, by Taylor Young.

Topic: A collection of laugh out loud humorous and outrageous deeds, based on true stories.

Description: From time to time it's entertaining to watch others squirm in hot water. The mean streak in us loves stories of woe – especially when it involves someone else. Sometimes, we are the blundering idiots with a tale of despair for others to be pleased about. Either way, the good deeds that don't go unpunished make such juicy stories!

Why You Can't See God, by David Lavy.

Topic: Is there real evidence for God's existence?

Description: One of the most provocative and to-the-point dialogues broached on this topic in years. No one can have a neutral reaction to this book; you'll either applaud its audacity or be disgusted by it, crass language and all. You may wonder whether fans of Mr. Lavy's book are in short supply, judging by some of the online jabs. What is all the fuss about, anyway? Is it really as bad as they say, or has a big ol' nerve been struck?

Boiled Down Money Goo, Tips For Propelling Your Financial Future, by Daniel and Deborah Minteer.

Topic: Lighthearted, fun, and to-the-point summaries of personal finance topics (the "cleaned up" version of Money Prick).

Description: Boiled Down Money Goo is a painless way to learn about a sometimes painful subject - personal finances. With a dose of humor to help it sink in, these simple, boiled down personal finance tips will outfit you in the best possible gear to weather the financial mudslides. While grandma may give similar advice, we won't dump it on your plate along with a lumpy bran and prune muffin...or flash any dentures.

****

About Taylor Young

Seattle, Washington native Taylor Young is a musician, engineer, book author, and family man.

"I love writing, whether song lyrics, technical papers, ranting in a blog, or more thought out topics worthy of a book. It is remarkable that writers today have a voice through online publishing. So much more time is freed up for letting the creative juices flow, which instead used to be spent pursuing and persuading publishers. The world benefits from this new freedom and I'm glad to be a part of it."

Contact Taylor at tyoung395@hotmail.com